DESTINATION AWESOME

DESTINATION AWESOME

Get the life you want
Even if you have to beat the odds

AMIEE MUELLER

New York

DESTINATION AWESOME

Get the life you want Even if you have to beat the odds

Published in New York, New York, by Morgan James Publishing. Morgan James and The Entrepreneurial Publisher are trademarks of Morgan James, LLC.
www.MorganJamesPublishing.com

The Morgan James Speakers Group can bring authors to your live event. For more information or to book an event visit The Morgan James Speakers Group at www.TheMorganJamesSpeakersGroup.com.

A free eBook edition is available with the purchase of this print book.

CLEARLY PRINT YOUR NAME ABOVE IN UPPER CASE

Instructions to claim your free eBook edition:
1. Download the BitLit app for Android or iOS
2. Write your name in **UPPER CASE** on the line
3. Use the BitLit app to submit a photo
4. Download your eBook to any device

ISBN 978-1-63047-503-1 paperback
ISBN 978-1-63047-504-8 eBook
Library of Congress Control Number:
2014920836

Cover Design by:
Rachel Lopez
www.r2cdesign.com

Interior Design by:
Bonnie Bushman
bonnie@caboodlegraphics.com

In an effort to support local communities and raise awareness and funds, Morgan James Publishing donates a percentage of all book sales for the life of each book to Habitat for Humanity Peninsula and Greater Williamsburg.

Get involved today, visit
www.MorganJamesBuilds.com

Habitat
for Humanity®
Peninsula and
Greater Williamsburg
Building Partner

TABLE OF CONTENTS

ACKNOWLEDGMENTS AND SINCERE THANKS

There are many people involved when getting a book ready for publication. Each plays an important role and deserves to be recognized for his or her contribution.

Thank you A.J., Jon, John, Denise, Lindsay, Gail, and Heather for your technical guidance and honest opinions.

Thank you Roy, Julian, Ryan, Patton, Chuck, Aaron, Loyd, Brett, Marc, Waseem, Aiden, and Yasemin for sharing your stories with me so I could share them with the world.

Thank you Josh for supporting me and believing in me. You are the highlight of all of my days.

To my family, thank you for letting me share our secrets and mistakes knowing it could make us look bad but could also help others feel or be better.

INTRODUCTION FROM THE AUTHOR

One of my most memorable Thanksgivings was spent eating fries and searching for an alcoholic. I was eight-years-old and my mom and her husband drove more than thirty miles from their home in Goshen, Indiana to pick up my brother and me to spend the holiday with them.

After they arrived, my step-dad shared a bottle of whiskey with my dad. Offering alcohol to an alcoholic was not one of my dad's better ideas. My step-dad was so obliterated when it was time to leave, my mom had to drive.

By the time we made it back to Goshen, Mom was fed up with his drunkenness. She drove to the house they shared with his parents, reached across him to open the passenger side door from within the car, lifted her right leg, like a dog at a fire hydrant, and pushed him out of the car with her foot. Then, she drove off with us kids and a mission to find some Thanksgiving dinner.

Because of the holiday, most businesses were closed. The only open restaurant we could find was Long John Silver's. After much protest from us about eating fish, Mom ordered us fries and soda for dinner. No turkey, no stuffing, no mashed potatoes or pie—never mind the warm feelings of togetherness I assumed most families shared on Thanksgiving.

I looked around the empty restaurant and it was clear that most families were not having fries and soda for dinner. I felt sad. This was nothing like the happy family gatherings I'd seen on TV or heard kids talk about at school. I felt deprived of more than nutritious food.

After our carborrific meal, we headed back to her in-laws' house only to discover that no one had seen my step-dad since we dropped him off. Then began the frantic search for the missing alcoholic. After 30 minutes of running up and down the street and in and out of other people's yards in the dark, his father found him in the spare bathroom, passed out on the toilet with his pants down and mouth hanging wide open.

If you haven't already guessed, holidays in my family were as far from awesome or a Hallmark movie as you could get. Don't get me wrong; I don't think I have the most appalling of families. I've heard enough tragic stories to know my upbringing could have been far worse. If you judged them solely by their friendliness, my family would rate pretty well. However, my childhood experiences weren't conventional. Only taking into account my siblings, parents, parents' siblings and my cousins, we have multiples of each: high school drop-outs, alcoholics, drug addicts, those who were in and out of jail, victims of molestation, teenage pregnancies, bankruptcies, government entitlement recipients and divorces. Remarriages. And divorces again.

Raised by my truck-driving dad in a trailer park, I had little knowledge of the world outside my town. Other than occasional ride-a-longs in my dad's eighteen-wheeler, up to the time I was fourteen, I had never done any travel outside of northern Indiana. I had never been to a play, musical, opera, or Broadway-type show. I couldn't have told you who the president was, who Michelangelo was, what cable TV was, or that the salad fork is usually the fork furthest from the plate.

Thinking back, it's possible some people looked at me back then and thought, "Poor kid. She'll be lucky if she makes it anywhere." They might have thought my future was set, determined by unfortunate circumstances. They might have assumed the odds were stacked too high against me, there was no hope for a bright future or a different path.

They would have been wrong.

My life may have been unfortunate up to that point, but it didn't have to be tragic. I may have been born into some crappy circumstances, but it didn't mean I couldn't make an awesome life for myself. It did mean, however, that I'd have to beat the odds to do it.

I know how it feels to be on my own, to have multiple areas in which to improve, to have a vision for a better lifestyle while not having all of the answers on how to bring it to fruition. I understand the sensation of being both scared and excited for the future. From trailer park to success story, not only did I put myself through college, graduate at the top of my class, move into a great career after college, succeed at a high level and earn a great income, I also nurtured wonderful relationships and developed myself along the way. I defied the odds, created the life I envisioned as a young person, and have been able to give back to others and help them do the same.

Through my own experience as well as mentoring and coaching hundreds of young adults in my career, I know, without a doubt, it is absolutely possible to move up the ladder of career, wealth, and fulfillment regardless of past or current circumstances.

This book is a compilation of stories that illuminate how I went from being an angry, untrusting, poor, socially-inept person with zero self-esteem to a happy, loving, confident, financially secure business professional with good friends, a better-than-I-could-have-ever-dreamed-of spouse, quality connections, stronger relationships with my family, and a passion for helping others absorb the lessons from which I've benefitted. You'll read many stories throughout these pages of my own experiences as well as those of others who have made significant, positive changes in their lives. I wrote this book to help you do it too.

What is Destination Awesome? It is a physical place for some. For me, it was a place far away from the trailer park—a safer, cleaner place with more energy and opportunity. For most, it is an emotional place. Destination Awesome is a way of living and a way of being. For you, it could be creating a life you love; an awesome life, or it could be about creating a you that you love; an awesome self. For me, it was all of the above. I dreamt of being a happy person in a life and place I loved. When that is the goal, what other word describes it better than *awesome?*

No matter where you are right now you can have more. Even if you think you will have to beat the odds to get to your Destination Awesome, I will show you how.

In this book I share simple concepts that are easy to implement. In fact, most chapters have bullet points to highlight the keys of each lesson as well as one *Gone In 600 Seconds* action step you can take. The reason for its title is each step can be performed in ten minutes or less and will help you leave the place you are now and put you on the path for the place you desire to be. If images of Nicolas Cage and Angelina Jolie pop into your head, just imagine they are two more supporters urging you forward. Angelina said once, "No matter what you have gone through in your youth, it is about who you choose to be in life. You can define your own destiny. You can be stronger than a very difficult past and overcome it."

I can truly say that I have never seen someone implement the methods in this book and not see improvement. I know if you commit to these strategies, you will make progress too. Take a step toward the future you desire by completing the suggested activity at the end of each chapter. Each exercise is included at the back of the book in the *Destination Awesome Action Guide*, along with resources that will help you move confidently toward your destination. Don't mistake the simplicity of each lesson for a lack of effectiveness. Every small step is progress. Each of these concepts had a big impact on me as well as the others you'll learn about. They are simple, but they are powerful.

I'm proof it doesn't matter where you come from, how much money you start out with, what misfortunes you've experienced, or what social circle you're born into. No matter your circumstances or the odds, you can make the life you desire for yourself by following simple success principles. Just as I did, you can go somewhere awesome, even if you feel like you are currently not on its path. You get on that path by simply choosing to take the first step.

Chapter 1

WHAT IS YOUR AWESOME?

One day when I was in fourth grade, I was sitting at my desk in class as our teacher, Mrs. Park, walked around the room handing back completed assignments. She'd lay the papers on each student's desk, and as they found out what grade they were given, my classmates would either be disappointed or relieved. We were given one of four marks: a plus, a check, a minus, or a circle minus. A minus was bad, and you really didn't want to get the circle minus, which was the worst.

Mrs. Park was behind me in the aisle and as she walked by my desk, she put my paper in front of me, which had an oversized plus on it. She said, "Good job. You should think about going to college."

She didn't stop to say it. It was just a casual comment she made as she kept moving to the next student, but it was the first time I remember hearing the word *college*. At 9-years-old, I didn't even really understand what it meant, but it felt like she said something positive about my future. I thought, "I don't know what college is, but I'm going to go there!"

On my journey, my first destination—my first awesome—was going to college. I had other goals in my life along the way, and have had many since, but this was the first choice I made for myself designed to get me out of the life I was living and into a better future.

The details of your desired destination may be quite different from mine, but if you want to improve some aspects of your life, the goal is the same.

Do you know where you want to go in life—what you want to see, and do, and feel? Maybe you want to experience things and gain insights by *living* them rather than reading or hearing about them. Maybe you know deep down that the path you're on will not take you there. Maybe money is tight. Maybe you don't have the support of friends or family. Maybe you've surrounded yourself with people who are content with life as is. Maybe you're not sure how to create the lifestyle you dream about. And maybe, because of how you were raised or the culture you grew up in, you don't believe it's possible for you to forge a new path. My goal is to help you turn those maybes into answers.

What do you want? When you look deep down inside, what is in your heart? Do you want to develop deeper relationships or enhance other social aspects of your life? Our connection with others has a huge impact on our happiness. Wanting to develop new, quality relationships or the depth of relationships you already have are both worthwhile and totally attainable.

Do you want to improve your health? It's normal to desire to feel stronger and more energetic. Your energy level has an impact on nearly everything else you do.

Maybe you want to increase your job enjoyment or academic success? Do you want to be wealthier? Happier? More confident? Maybe like I did, you want to travel more. Visiting places all around the world has been a highlight for me.

Your desires may be related to your past. Do you want to let go of discomforts from your history or find a way to forgive a hurt caused by someone else? These aims can be a powerful way to enhance your future.

As you move forward in in this book it's helpful to have at least one awesome destination in mind. Rarely do things go perfectly and rarely are valuable outcomes easy to achieve. Just as an airplane continually adjusts its route to stay on track to its destination, we need a destination to measure against in order to make those needed adjustments or decisions.

There is no correct or incorrect Destination Awesome. Whatever you'd need to achieve in order to feel like you've reached your awesome destination, that is what you should have in mind as your end goal.

Though your particular destination will be unique to you, let's look at a few areas that many of us tend to consider when we think about what would be awesome for ourselves. While I do that, I wouldn't be giving you the whole story if I didn't share the odds you'll have to beat to reach awesomeness in those areas.

Many of us relate awesome to the idea of having a career we love. One that we are excited to go to each day. Not one where we are simply trading time for money. StatisticBrain.com, an on-line stats resource whose mission is to provide accurate and timely statistics, reports more than 70% of Americans experience physical and mental symptoms caused by stress; the *American Psychological Association* reports Americans consistently experience stress levels higher than is healthy. One of the top three types of stress is work-related stress. In a *CBS News* report, 70% of Americans said they are unhappy at work, mostly because they don't feel engaged or passionate about what they are doing.

The odds say you are unlikely to be supremely happy at work or stress free when it comes to your work.

When envisioning an awesome life, many of us also think of our lifestyle as it relates to money. How great does it sound to be financially worry free? To know the money is there for the bills, to have the ability to travel, take time off, invest in an opportunity when it presents itself, or to be able to give to great causes, charities or people in need? Lifestyle is most often synonymous with wealth, though it would be shortsighted to think money is the only variable in true wealth.

Based on 2010-2011 information from the Internal Revenue Service (IRS), the U.S. Census Bureau, and the Federal Reserve, the *Statistic Brain* reported the average American family has less than $4,000 in total savings and that half of us have none put away for retirement, which describes the vast majority of my family. Wow! Those numbers certainly do not provide for much in the way of freedom, options or an ability to donate to charity. In order to beat the odds financially, you'll have to either have a much higher income than average or better financial management habits than most. Or both.

People Who Have Shown Us You Can Beat the Odds

- Guy Laliberte was a street performer before introducing the world to Cirque du Soleil, which is hugely successful. The company became the largest theatrical producer in the world with over nineteen shows in nearly 300 cities, including some permanent productions in Las Vegas, employing more than 4,000 people, generating revenues of more than $800,000,000 a year and winning multiple awards and distinctions.

- Climbing from the housing projects of Brooklyn to the CEO of Starbucks with a personal net worth of over one billion is the story of Howard Schultz, who in 2012, was listed in *Forbes* as one of the 400 wealthiest people in the U.S.

- Leonardo Del Vecchio went from being an orphaned factory worker to an apprentice for a tool and dye maker, to the founder of the largest manufacturer of sunglasses (including Ray-Ban and Oakley) and prescription glasses. As of 2011, he was ranked as the second wealthiest person in all of Italy and the seventy-first wealthiest person in the world.

- J.K. Rowling was a single mother living on welfare when she wrote the first book of the famous *Harry Potter* series. That series went on to win many awards, sell more than 400,000,000 copies, and be the base of the highest grossing film series in history. The movies have generated more than eleven billion in consumer spending when taking into account both theater sales and home viewing revenue.

- Oprah went from wearing potato sacks for dresses to working in radio while in high school to co-anchoring a local news broadcast to being one of the most well-known, influential and financially successful women on the planet. Her program was the highest rated talk show ever. There's no need to even give her last name for everyone knows to whom I'm referring.

In addition to career and finances, many of us equate awesomeness to having relationships that bring us happiness and fulfillment. In fact, in more than 250 studies done on happiness, the common theme, when considering all of the external factors that affect our happiness levels, is that it is related more to our connections with others than anything else. Yet nearly 50% of all marriages end in divorce and close to another 20% of people never marry. Taking into account divorce and never tying the knot, that's around 70% of people who may lack one of the most fulfilling types of relationships.

Spending quality time with people is important in relationships. The Bureau of Labor Statistics reports on the ways the average American workers allot their time. The Bureau found that after sleep, work, grooming, eating, household activities and caring for family, just over four hours a day is left for leisure and athletic activities. When you couple that with surveys of Americans and the Nielsen Co. reporting that the average American is watching five hours of TV and video a day, there is little to no time left for cultivating friendships.

To have the awesome relationships you desire, you will have to beat those odds.

What Can You Do to Beat the Odds?

A helpful step in beating the career odds is to do your research. While studies show that having a degree still leads to a higher likelihood of getting work than not having a degree, they also tell us that some majors have higher employment rates than others.

A 2013 study by Georgetown University's Center on Education and the Workforce shows a better employment rate for graduates of nursing, elementary education, and chemistry and lower employment rates for graduates of information systems, architecture, and film, video, and photography arts. Whether higher education is part of your plan or not, you'll find suggestions in this book on how to beat the career and financial odds in chapters covering topics such as positioning yourself, finding a beneficial network, trust levels and being better than average.

Getting to your awesome also requires you make better choices. With a lagging economy, rising cost of living, uncertainty in governmental policy and spending, and easy access to substances and casual sex, decisions are coming with tougher consequences than in years past. With people struggling to make ends meet, an unplanned pregnancy would be even more challenging. With competition for jobs increasing, due to both global access and a high unemployment rate in the U.S., skipping class or blowing off schoolwork and the resulting effect on a transcript or the possible lengthening of time in school may have a larger impact on you than students of previous generations. Overall, and as unfair as it is, you will need to make better decisions than your parents did. Many chapters cover this topic in the personal characteristics and behavior portions of this book.

You will have to build beneficial relationships. With the average household in America comprised of either a single parent or two working parents, which leads to less family time, young adults need to be able to find mentors and supportive peer groups. You'll find information in this book related to this topic; nearly a third of it is committed to helping you build valuable relationships.

Also key to beating the odds is a commitment to continued learning. The world is changing more quickly than ever before and we have to be more adaptable. Continued growth in skills and knowledge is the way to build your adaptability. The great news is resources for learning are abundant. Just reading this book is a notch on the learning belt so kudos to you for picking it up.

Brendon Burchard—one of the highest paid trainers in the world—has read a book every week for many years. His commitment to continued growth is inspiring, and it is easy to see that it has paid off for him. So once you are done with this book, pick up another, or watch a documentary, set up a lunch with a professional in an industry in which you are interested, attend an event at which a speaker shares insights, get a study group together, or any of the many other ways you can cultivate learning.

In the coming pages, you'll read about the shortcomings I grew up with, but it's important to understand that at some point, when I got old enough, the choice between continuing to live unchanged and traveling a different path was mine alone. If I was still living that lifestyle, I wouldn't be able to point the finger at my parents, at my lack of money or skills, or at other people's expectations of me. We are all the captains of our own ships.

My dad was a single parent and a high school dropout with very few career options. He took the highest paying job he could get—truck driving—which kept him away from home 90% of the time. The very little time I spent with him, I saw how hard he worked, how tired he was, how limited his time was with my brother and me and how little he had to show for it. I looked around the trailer park and thought, "There has to be a better way."

How did other people have a more joyful existence, and what did I need to do to be one of them rather than one of us?

The only answer I came up with early on was education. I was fortunate to have a passion for learning whatever could help me improve my situation. Neither of my parents or my siblings finished high school. My mom and my brother eventually received their GEDs, but education was something no one in my family had much of or seemed to care much about. My teachers and people on television claimed education could be transforming. McGruff the Crime Dog would pop into the commercials telling me to stay in school and a public service announcement touted, "If you want to be cool, stay in school." Michael Jordan talked about the importance of education. Teachers, television, and famous athletes all shared the same advice about the importance of education, and that is what I latched on to.

Academic education started me down my path. It wouldn't be until many years later I'd be subjected to the wisdom of leaders living lives of success and fulfillment. From them, I'd learn education doesn't end with a diploma or even college degrees. That is when my focus shifted to personal and professional growth which led me to a place, physically and mentally, far away from the trailer park.

Jim Rohn worked for more than forty years as an author, speaker and personal development trainer who helped people all over the world sculpt life strategies. He said, "Formal education will make you a living; self education will make you a fortune." That fortune can be a wealth of money, great relationships, happiness, and freedom. Not many people strive for lots of money for the funds alone; it's about what good they can do with the money and the freedom it provides. Adam Stock, the founder of Rising Stock, a profitability coaching company, said, "Money can't buy you happiness, but neither can poverty. So why not be rich?"

I've shared a lot of numbers and information, and you may feel a bit overwhelmed at this point, maybe even a bit discouraged. I want you to know, without a doubt, that no matter how far it is to your Destination Awesome, you can make it. There is no far that is too far. We arrive at some destinations quicker than others. We arrive at some ready to celebrate and at others ready to nap. Maybe this process comes easily to you; maybe you're ready for this book and are at the exact right place in your life to take action. Maybe you'll have to work through it slowly and deliberately, like you're cutting a path through a jungle of brush as tall as you using a dull-edged machete. Either way, you will make it. If you keep going, keep taking action, and keep swinging your blade, you will make it. So my question for you is, "Where are you going?"

Vehicles to Take You to
AWESOME

Begin by thinking about the big picture of your future. We'll break it into smaller, more immediate goals or milestones soon, but first you want to have an ultimate destination (or characteristics of a destination) in mind. Whether on paper, in the margins of this page or just in your mind, it will help to answer the following questions.

What type of work would be awesome to do? You can write down career titles or simply any traits you desire such as flexibility of schedule, travel, working on a team or using creativity.

What is your financial awesome? What do you want to be able to do with your money?

Describe what you believe makes for awesome relationships. Is it a number of friends you'd like to have? Consistent or quality communication? Openness and sharing? Lack of conflict? Common goals or interests?

In regards to your personal development, what would be awesome to you? What would you really like to learn at some point? How to build a website, a car engine, a tree house, or a financial portfolio? Do you want to improve in dancing, singing, painting, or driving a manual car?

Gone In 600 Seconds

Now break it down a bit further, and make a list of any changes you'd like to make over the next six months. Don't limit your answers. Use this time to brainstorm. You can evaluate priorities of the list later. You'll soon discover that improving one area will automatically help you begin to improve others.

You'll also find this exercise, and others, in the Destination Awesome Action Guide at the back of the book.

Example list of changes to make in the next six months:

Improve GPA

Lose weight

Improve communication skills

Make new friends

Save money

Learn to do all household chores

Read more

Change jobs

Join a group or club

Create a study group for each class

Chapter 2

DAMAGE DOESN'T HAVE TO BE PERMANENT

R oy grew up knowing his family would not be able to pay for higher education, so he followed in his older brother's footsteps and joined the military after high school. He knew he'd be able to use their GI bill program to go to school once he finished his time in the Marine Corps. So at age 17, he enlisted.

One evening, a couple of years later, Roy and two other guys from his regiment decided to go out and have some fun. At the door of the bar, Roy realized he left his ID in the car so he went back to get it and his friends went inside. After closing the car door and heading back toward the bar with ID in hand, he heard a woman cry out, "Please help me!"

Heeding strict military rules regarding any involvement with civilians, Roy kept walking. But then he heard it again.

"Help me. He's going to kill me!"

Roy stopped walking, turned to where the screams were coming from and saw a large man beating on a woman. So he walked over to where they were tussling and asked him, "Hey man, why don't you stop? Maybe you two should separate and calm down."

The man, clearly drunk, wasn't happy Roy was intruding in their personal business. He advanced on Roy, dishing out threats. So Roy punched him, and though he didn't mean to, he knocked him out. The man fell to the ground. Out cold.

Thinking the woman with bruises and cuts on her face was out of harm's way, Roy turned to join his friends in the bar. As he approached the door, he was jumped from behind. The woman, also drunk, tackled him and started hitting him and yelling, "You killed my boyfriend!" She scratched and slapped him, and he couldn't get her off of his back.

A few other men at the bar door saw her wounds and thought Roy was the culprit, and did what they felt was heroic: they joined in kicking Roy's butt. One guy grabbed a bottle and hit Roy in the head with it, drawing blood. Then after noticing the bottle was broken, he thrust it at Roy's chest. Turning to protect his chest, the bottle lodged in Roy's arm and opened another wound. Blood began to gush from his arm.

With his injured arm, Roy grabbed the guy who stabbed him by his long hair and held him down, while the other men continued to pummel him. By that time, people inside the bar noticed a commotion and came pouring out into the parking lot to see the action. That's when Roy's friends found out what was going on. Once they stepped in to even the odds, there was no comparison. The marines were going to take the title.

Moments later the police arrived. They asked what had happened and who was to blame. All fingers pointed to Roy. Initially the cops thought Roy severely injured the man with the long hair, but came to realize it was just Roy's blood all over the man's head. The cops also thought it was Roy who had done the damage to the woman. They handcuffed him and were preparing to haul him away when a man, from the business across the street from the bar, came walking over. He had seen the entire conflict and put the police straight on what happened, beginning with how Roy stepped in to help the lady who was being beaten by her boyfriend.

The police let Roy out of the cuffs. Knowing the military police would not approve of the situation, regardless of his intentions, Roy and his friends decided not to tell them, which also meant not seeking medical attention. Roy's friend pulled the bottle from his arm, dumped alcohol on it, and scotch-taped the wound closed.

The evening of the fight, Roy's perspective changed. He decided no good deed goes unpunished. Essentially, don't get involved, even if someone needs help, because it's likely to come back to bite you. And though he wouldn't admit it to his comrades, he was hesitant to go out again for fear of ending up in a similar situation. To his friends, he just said he didn't have the money to go out. So for the few months it took his hesitation to subside, they stayed in and played cards.

Have you ever experienced something that took such a toll on you that you wondered if you'd ever get over it? Was it physical damage, an injury or illness you weren't sure would ever heal? Was it heartache or disappointment that cut so deep you thought it might ache forever? Maybe it was a perspective shift, something that changed the way you see the world and not necessarily for the better. Have you wondered if there is anything you can do to put it behind you and leave it there?

Years later, Roy was a student of Karate and was injured badly when he was kicked in the back. After quite of bit of time on prescription drugs, which made him feel groggy and failed to ease his pain, a friend recommended he see a chiropractor. Knowing nothing about chiropractic adjustment, but desperate for a solution, he took his friend's advice.

"I was drug free and jogging four weeks later," Roy told me. "It was a life changing experience for me. That chiropractor helped me so much, and it was just the coolest thing I'd ever seen. It lit a fire underneath me." That was when Roy set his sights on chiropractic school.

Today, Roy is the owner of a successful chiropractic and nutrition company. He has been the associate team chiropractor to the University of Texas Athletic Program in Austin for the past twenty years and helps athletes recover from injuries. His entire career centers around helping people, and usually when he's sharing his success stories with me, they are about the clients he has helped avoid surgeries by using joint, muscle, and alignment therapies.

Oftentimes, an old injury or pain we suffered leaves remnants such as a scar or residue of a once deeply held perspective, and it is up to us to recognize it as just a lingering reminder of our experience and not as a permanent viewpoint or debility.

Roy told me that recently he let some junior high neighborhood boys play basketball in his driveway when they asked to use his hoop. While they were playing, they accidentally broke a mirror off of one of his cars. He had an instant thought flashback of, "No good deed goes unpunished," but at least now, that phrase makes him chuckle.

Since situations still arise that support the perspective that helping others may result in your own detriment, I asked him how he handles it now and why he decides to still help people when there is a chance he could suffer negative consequences. He said some of his perspective came with maturity, but mostly, "If I don't do what I feel is right, then I won't feel good about myself. If I do something mean or negative or if I don't help someone who needs it, I'll feel bad."

The worth of helping someone isn't based on the ultimate outcome. It's worth doing because it feels good to be helpful. After the bar brawl incident, Roy could have lived a damaged life, not helping people, had he let his initial perspective on it persist. Instead, Roy's arm eventually healed and so did his mindset. Although he will probably never step into a parking lot fight again, he went back to being himself—a guy with a passion to help others live healthier, less painful lives.

The great news, for all of us, is pain or damage doesn't have to be permanent. The bad news is that it can be, if we let it.

Have you ever heard someone say, "Pain doesn't hurt?" Well, it does hurt, but it isn't always bad. Sometimes pain can be a good thing. If I don't feel some sort of pain when I'm working out or the next day, I tend to think I didn't work out hard enough. Instead of thinking of pain as a result, think of it as a signal, a sign your attention is needed in order to affect a result or fix a problem. A *temporary* problem. If you can implement that perspective, you can work through and overcome anything.

We've all been hurt in some way; we each have our own scars. But while scars may be permanent, the way we view the world doesn't have to be.

A Bar Fight and a Birthmark

It was the morning after one of my grandma's most intense bar fights, and she and my mom were sitting on the couch. My grandma stopped by to *show and tell* my mom about her experience the previous evening. When Mom looked at her mother, what she saw caused the most intense shiver she ever experienced to crawl down her spine.

At that time, my maternal grandmother was a thin, attractive woman standing no taller than five foot two with short, brunette hair curled and puffed. Throughout her life, people had commented on her prettiness. She had a big, bright smile and deep, brown eyes. To look at her, you might believe she was demure, but that would only last until you had a conversation. She was as feisty as she was petite. Her name was Dorothy, and I would know her as Grandma Dot.

Dot grew up in Alabama. She met her first love, Gordon, when she was thirteen. He was older and would offer her stolen cigarettes and candy from the small convenience stores he frequented. Their courtship led to her 60-year smoking habit and their nuptials when she was 14. She was passionately in love with Gordon and was devastated when just seven years after they married, he fell off a roof at work and died leaving her a widow and single mother of three.

After a brief second marriage, and divorce, she took her kids to live in Goshen, Indiana where she met and married her third husband Paul. Paul's son Tooter brought a friend home from work one day, and that friend met Dot's daughter. That friend was my dad and that daughter was my mom, and that was how their story began.

During Dot's residence in Indiana, she was in her forties, my mom had already given birth to my older brother, was pregnant with her second child—me—and my family was living in a trailer park on Highway 87.

Dot and Paul were regular customers of a bar in Goshen named Riverview. When Dot went out, drinking was a customary part of the experience. At this establishment alone, she had been in four separate drunken bar fights. One of which had occurred the night before she visited my pregnant mother. As they sat on the couch, she shared what she could recall of the bar fight the night before. My mom asked what started the quarrel. Dot couldn't remember that bit of information, but she had no trouble recollecting one small part of the fight as it left her with a painful reminder. Dot slowly lifted a clump of hair to show my mom a nickel-sized patch of red skin on the left side of her head, which was full of hair a day earlier and was now bare. Her opponent had ripped a chunk of hair away. That was the moment my mom experienced the penetrating shiver.

The most bizarre twist in the story is months later I was born with a bald spot on the left side of my head. It is still bald today, and I expect it always will be. The doctor said the most likely cause of my bald spot was my head rested against something in the womb, but that story isn't nearly as much fun for my family to tell as the legendary bar fight and infamous shiver.

I share this story with you to give you a sense of my family's conduct, and also because while I contemplate the many life lessons I've learned since leaving the trailer park, including not to get on Dot's bad side, I'm grateful the characteristics of the past are not determining factors of the future. Whether they are historical traits of a person's perspective, behaviors, results, circumstances, or limitations is irrelevant because all of those things can be changed.

Dot didn't let the heartache from losing her first husband stop her from finding another great love. I didn't let my childhood lifestyle keep me from aiming for something greater, and Roy didn't let his experience of being cut by being helpful dissuade him from a career in helping people.

Letting Go

Reframing is a common technique people have used to not only let go of past damage but also find a way to turn their pain into a benefit. When something happens to us, we have a way of looking at it, a perspective of our situation. Changing that perspective is reframing it. For example, when a girl gets dumped, her perspective might be that it is the end of the world. That she may never love again or find a person better suited for her than the one who just left. An alternative perspective would be that she is better off. That her ex leaving was just what she needed to find her soul mate. Of course, these perspectives are not gender specific. Guys share similar perspective choices.

Our perspective or frame of reference is, in fact, a choice. The way we look at our situation is within our control. Let's say two men are sitting in the stands of a football game and it's fifty degrees outside. One man mentions he wishes he had brought a thicker jacket; it's colder than he expected. The other man, wearing only a thin jersey, gives his friend a weird look. He's so warm he offers his jersey to him saying he'd be content to be shirtless in such warm weather. How can two people have the same experience and totally different points of view?

Maybe the first man grew up in an Arizona city where it rarely hits temperatures below seventy degrees, while the second man grew up in the upper peninsula of Michigan for which the average low, even in summer, rarely gets above fifty degrees. What they are used to or their point of reference has an impact on their current assessment. Is fifty degrees warm or cold? There isn't a right or wrong answer since it depends on your perspective of that temperature—a perspective you get to choose. For example, I grew up in the north, where the temperature rarely rose above fifty degrees for months, and I still think anything below sixty is cold. Just because we experience a lot of something doesn't mean we can't make an independent or unusual assessment of how we feel about it.

Positive reframing involves taking a way of looking at a situation and shifting it so it is helpful, not hurtful. Wallowing in break-up grief rarely, if ever, benefits the wallower. I'm not saying people should never be sad, but the time to move on does come. The girl who thought her world was over can reframe her new single status as an opportunity to find an even better relationship. When she thinks differently about it, she will feel differently about it. When she thinks optimistically, the likelihood of good things coming her way increases.

There are many examples and studies of how people's views of situations plays a major role in their happiness and ability to move forward effectively despite any damage they've suffered. One key to getting past any hurt is dealing with it. Avoiding it, trying to block it out or pretending it never happened is not a pathway to healing. Working through it is a necessary part of the process.

Do Your Past or Current Circumstances Hold You Back?

Most people have heard the saying, "The past does not equal the future." It most certainly doesn't. I am eager to spread the idea that not only does the past not equal the future, but neither does the present. If there are areas of your life you'd like to change or improve, there is no doubt it is possible for you to achieve that goal.

What I love about *now* is it's temporary. Regardless of where you come from or where you are—physically, mentally, socially, spiritually, or professionally—you can get to where you'd rather be. What happened in the past is over. What's happening now is impermanent. What happens in the future is up to you.

In chapter 1, you read about a handful of examples of people who came from limited pasts—the kind of pasts that convince some, in similar situations, that their future is bleak because of it. And you know, through their examples, the past does not have to define the future.

The only thing from my past I carry with me permanently is my bald spot. Every other area of my life has experienced growth.

"No matter how well you know what a person has done and what he thought he was doing when he did it and what he now thinks of what he did, it is impossible to be certain of what he will do next."

—Orson Scott Card

When dealing with a situation that is causing negative emotions such as fear, frustration, sadness or anger, ask yourself, "How can this benefit me?" or "What can I learn from this that will positively impact my future?"

Look to others. If you are struggling to overcome a pain or damaging experience, look for others who have experienced something similar and overcame it. Reach out to them and ask them to tell you about their story. Also ask them how they came through it successfully.

Gone In 600 Seconds

Can you think of an experience you had that still causes negative emotions to creep in when you remember it? If so, give it a title. Roy's title could be "Bar Fight" for example.

Once you have the title written down, try to reframe your perspective on it. Think of ways to look at what happened that are different than the way you've always looked at it. This is not always an easy task. Sometimes, it takes courage and persistence to make the mental shift.

If you need an example, read chapter 8: *Trust Makes You Strong*. You'll learn about an experience I went through, the kind that has caused lifelong negative emotions for some with similar experiences, and you'll read how I reframed it for myself.

Read the *Destination Awesome Action Guide* at the back of the book for more exercises and resources.

Chapter 3

THE STARTING POINT

What would others say about you?

If you asked a variety of people to give honest feedback of their impressions of you—some who have spent a lot of time with you, some who only have first impressions to draw from, some you met in social, academic or work situations—what would they say? Asking for feedback is a great exercise, especially if you are looking for areas of improvement that may elude your self-evaluation. It's also interesting to see if your own perception of your impression on others aligns with theirs. If you use this exercise, I suggest you view any criticism with gratitude for gaining knowledge you can work with rather than anger or grief as a result of feedback that seems less than positive.

There is value in asking for feedback from others. It is so difficult to evaluate ourselves and whether or not we are letting others see our true selves, mainly because of two things: We are generally harder on ourselves than anyone else, and we can't read other people's minds.

During the conception of this book, I reached out to a handful of people who knew me before my period of considerable growth. I thought it would be interesting to find out what other people's impressions of me were at a time when

I would describe myself as a mess. I can tell you what I thought of myself, but so often what we think of ourselves and what others think of us don't match.

I sent these individuals a message asking for their true opinions of me back then. I wanted the good and the bad. I let them know I would not be offended and didn't want them to hold back. You'll see their responses in this chapter, and I only ask that you consider what type of impression those responses give you of who I was then. By reading their opinions and adding it to my own, you'll have a good idea of my starting place, from which I began my journey to a happier life.

A Life Map

If at birth we were each given a map to our life's happiness and success—to Destination Awesome—our choices would be much easier. If such a map exists, the hospital forgot to send one home with my parents. They were out of pink blankets when I came into the world, so I was wrapped in blue. Maybe they were out of maps too.

In my own trials and travels, I've discovered three different routes to get you from where you are now to where you want to be. For me, it was necessary to travel all three. You may only need one to achieve your goals, but I will share all three so you can decide what makes sense for you. Implementing ideas from any or all three can set you free and keep you from ever having to return to a place you don't want to be.

The three routes are: The Road Paved in Relationships, The Path of Personal Characteristics and the Boulevard of Behavior.

The Road Paved in Relationships is about your connection with others. You may have heard someone say something like, "It's not what you know, it's whom you know." Though that statement isn't all encompassing, there is some truth to it. Charlie Jones, author of *Life is Tremendous* of which more than 2,000,000 copies were printed, once said, "You will be the same person in five years as you are today except for the people you meet and the books you read." I believe he meant relationships and knowledge are paramount factors in your growth.

Cultivating relationships was an enormous weakness of mine the entire time I was in school. I didn't know how to communicate with people, how to treat people, or how to develop good relationships. I met Lisa Gingerich in fourth grade when she moved to my school, and we've been best friends ever since. I have no idea how I got so lucky that she'd be my BFF considering how awful I could be when we were kids and teenagers. Especially teenagers. Of course I asked Lisa to provide an opinion of how I was back then, and after being my closest friend for more than eight years, here is how she described me.

Lisa said, "Amiee always had to be right, and in fact, she was at most times. She always wanted others to see her correctness. It was like she would force her views on people. It is a wonderful thing to be smart and she has always been miles ahead of others in this area, but she had a tendency to be judgmental and overbearing. She was very quick to see the bad in others. Patience was not one of her strong suits. On occasion, she was not very caring toward others and their feelings."

On my journey of life changes, if it weren't for the people I met along the way I may never have gotten to this wonderful place of achievement. And even if I had, without connection to others, I definitely wouldn't feel fulfilled or happy. We thrive when he have positive connections with others.

I knew I was making progress when about two years after I began this journey, I was hanging out with Lisa. We were out, not doing anything particularly exciting, but we were crossing paths with other people who were also out that day. After witnessing a few of my interactions with these strangers, Lisa said to me, "You've really changed. I just want you to know that I notice, and it's great."

The Road Paved in Relationships includes the power of peers, the benefits of mentorship, your impact on others and the philosophy behind finding the good in people.

The Second Route

The second route to your desired life is The Path of Personal Characteristics, and it will show you how taking on certain traits will help you make your desired progress. Every über successful person I've heard from says *who you are* is more important than *what you do*. To get what you want, simply become a person who'd get it. One of my favorite quotes by Ralph Waldo Emerson is, "What lies behind us and what lies before us are tiny matters compared to what lies within us."

I'm sure you've already guessed, but I also had to work to develop some helpful characteristics as well as rid myself of self-doubt, having to be right all of the time, and mistrust of others. Two girls I went to school with have provided their opinions of me during that time.

Autumn Mynhier and I were not in the same circle of friends, but since my step-mom was friends with her mom, and her mom cut my hair, we crossed paths. Autumn said, "I have known Amiee since before elementary school, because our parents were friends. She was the quiet type. She played sports, but was never the star player. She had a group of girls that she hung out with—non-athletic, somewhat academic, but today they would be described as the invisible crowd and the have-nots. I am sure she had her fair share of being bullied or ridiculed for not wearing the current styles. I know Amiee has trialed through some tough times with her family; prison, divorce, poverty, and I am sure her parents did not expect her to go to college, pay for it herself, and move forward, toward living a better life than what she grew up in. She is an inspiration and success! Rags to riches one might say!"

Jessica Sutton and I were not close friends in high school, but we ended up at the same college and in the same dorm. After our first college semester, some girls left school and others got moved around in the dorm. It worked out that we roomed together for our second semester, so we got to know each other a lot better.

When I asked Jessica to describe me back then, she said, "It seemed to me in college she was kind of shy and had low self-esteem. Confident or risk-taker are not words most would use to describe her in high school. When she was younger, she didn't project happiness or a positive attitude."

The Path of Personal Characteristics includes lessons in trust, choosing your identity, overcoming fears and generating a thicker skin. For me, this route was the hardest to travel. It was sort of like going uphill, with a strong down wind while wearing roller skates. It was a tough trek, but now that I'm mostly on the other side of that hill, it's easy to see how the benefits are worth the grueling task. Each chapter related to this route will help you determine which traits you'd like to enhance in yourself and how to do it. Usually, we already possess the characteristics; we just need to strengthen them.

The first road is about your relationship with others and how it affects your outcomes. The second path is about your relationship with yourself and who you will be in order to achieve what you want. The last is about your actions, what you'll do to get to where you aspire to be. You must take action.

The Third Route

Behavior shifts are a bit easier than character shifts. Both are totally attainable, but character is such an internal mechanism whereas behavior is a little more related to the external. Our behaviors are the actions we take. I'm sure you've seen someone behave in a way that is out of the norm for him. For example, a shy person works up the nerve to speak to someone who makes him nervous. Maybe you've seen a person who normally behaves in a selfish manner unexpectedly do something nice for someone else. The actions we take are in the moment, whereas our characteristics are longer term. So actions are a little easier to change immediately. To make a true behavior shift, though, the action must be repeated until it becomes the norm, not the unexpected surprise.

Some of the behavioral changes I needed to make included being more open-minded to other people's opinions, having a more useful focus and adjusting my internal dialog. You can see that I was not the only one to think I needed to grow in these areas. Shalisa Troyer was one of the girls I spent a lot of time with in junior high and high school. She didn't live far from me, we were in the same grade, and we had a mutual friend who introduced us.

When I asked for her feedback of me back then, she said, "I thought she had to grow up too fast. She had to take on the motherly role at such a young age. Yes she could be grouchy at times, but now that I'm older, I can understand why she acted that way. She was grouchy when there were too many people around her doing dumb things."

Since I was paying my way through college, I looked for a job as soon as I got to my campus town. That's when I met Blake Chastain. He ended up being my first mentor. Here is what Blake said when describing me then: "When we met, Amiee was applying to work in my sales office. It was her first sales job outside of fundraisers for school. She was somewhat shy, skeptical, opinionated, and had a chip on her shoulder. She was always a by-the-book, black-and-white thinker with no grey areas. She was kind of negative but witty and extremely loyal to her friends. I believe she just wanted to be part of something or was still looking for something."

I am so fortunate that Blake gave me a position on his sales team. I owe him a lot for giving a skeptical, opinionated and shy girl a chance. It was that job that kick-started my growth-spurt and changed my life. Blake wasn't just a great mentor; he was the perfect mentor for me at that time in my life.

The Boulevard of Behavior includes how to move toward higher productivity, being better than average, having the right focus, positioning yourself for success, your self-talk and the sacrifices you'll need to think about. Each has had an impact on my success and happiness.

Now that you've seen others' opinions of me at my starting point (opinionated, shy, chip on the shoulder, and grouchy), do you have an impression of who I was back then? Did I sound like a person you'd want to spend time with? You'd want on your sporting team? Work team? Class project group? Most likely, you are thinking, "no way," and I don't blame you.

I understand, because that person wouldn't be my first pick either.

Now it's time to start moving you down the road to your own progress, and it's my pleasure to share the approaches that changed my life in every way so you can put them to use.

Vehicles to Take You to AWESOME

Good intentions aren't enough to redirect your path. Having a plan of what you will do differently is like having the car sitting in the driveway. Implementing that plan, of course, is driving that car. So, think through and write down the answers to the following.

Your Boulevard of Behaviors. What are 1-3 actions you can implement consistently that would help you achieve your awesome destination? For example, would it impact you positively to get up earlier, save a certain amount of money from each check, use a calendar for projects or school work, or drink less soda or eat less sugar?

Your Road Paved in Relationships. Take stock of your relationships. List the types of relationships you currently have such as romantic, family, work, school, friends, or others. Then think about what the relationships in each area would be like if they were what you'd consider awesome. From 1-10, rank how close they are now to your ideal vision for them. 0 being not at all like your ideal. 10 being exactly like your ideal. If they are not above 6, consider creating a plan for improvement including any behaviors you could implement that would help you with that goal.

Your Path of Personal Characteristics. List out the characteristics or traits you admire most in other people, such as trustworthy, confident, knowledgeable, generous, or funny. For a list of many traits to choose from, visit http://amieemueller.com/positive-characteristics-of-admirable-people/. List as many as you can think of or choose the ones you deem most important from the webpage. Then rank yourself from 1-10 (1 being it doesn't describe you at all, 10 being it is one of your greatest strengths). Star or circle ones you want to improve

26

first. How would your life be different if *you* had all of the characteristics you admire greatly in others?

Gone In 600 Seconds

Send messages to five to ten people asking for their opinions on your good qualities and areas for growth. Remember, the more diverse the group, the more well rounded the feedback. Giving a deadline will help with getting a reply in a timely fashion.

Further insights on how to use the feedback without letting it bring you down can be found the chapter titled *Dealing With Adversity*. You will also find this exercise and other related exercises in the *Destination Awesome Action Guide* at the back of the book.

Asking for Feedback—Sample message:

Hey Joe,

I am participating in a self-analysis project. I need to get feedback from a handful of people, and I'm hoping you can help, as I value your opinion. It will only take a few minutes.

Can you reply with the following:

Your impression of my strengths or good qualities

Your impression of my areas for growth or improvement

I am looking for total honesty. Don't worry about hurting my feelings. The only way you could upset me is by holding back. ☺

If you are able to do this and have it back to me by (one week from now), I'd really appreciate it.

Thanks,

(your name)

The Road Paved
in Relationships

Chapter 4

HOW PEERS IMPACT YOUR RESULTS

One sunny day, the windows were open, Dad's car was in the driveway, and we had a special visitor whose white van was parked on the gravel at the bottom of the drive. I was 8-years-old, holding a flyswatter, and my heartbeat was starting to pick up. One of the things I feared most was about to attack.

Our kitchen table was filled with bowls, plates, cups and other items which previously filled the now empty cabinets. The big man wearing rubber gloves and a tank on his back looked at my dad and me and asked if we were ready. The tank had a hose that led to a sprayer the man was holding in his right hand.

With a nod from my dad, the man turned a nozzle and began to spray, releasing a toxic liquid into the cabinets. Instantly hundreds of cockroaches fled their homes in our cupboards and ran straight at us. The job of squashing them with the flyswatters was entrusted to my dad and me, but my little arms were not very fast.

My heart was pounding and each time one of them would crawl on me, its hairy legs tickling my skin, a wave of revulsion swept over me. My focus was on keeping them off me, so my aim was for the ones closest to my body rather than swatting for the multitudes within reach but farther from my feet. Lots of the little buggers made it past me. That process went on for about five minutes before the number of runners began to dissipate. When the swatting stopped, our special bonus was cleaning the squished bodies off the cheap, yellowing linoleum.

For at least six years, we dealt with cockroach infestations. On the nights I'd get out of bed to use the bathroom, I'd flip the light switch and roaches would scatter for the security of darkness. Frequently, I had nightmares of roaches crawling on me while I slept. It was common to find dead ones in cabinets or in corners of the floor or kitchen counter. My dad had pest control treat the issue a few times, but it had not resolved.

That day I overheard him asking the man with the sprayer why we were failing in our extermination efforts. The man said, "They are coming in through the sewer, which is linked to your neighbors. So until everyone in the park treats the problem, it's going to be nearly impossible to get rid of them."

That was our answer. Our peers were affecting our results.

How Peers Affect Your Results

You've probably heard of peer pressure. Who hasn't?

It's a term thrown around a lot in our teenage years. Dictionary.com defines peer pressure as "the social pressure by members of one's peer group to take a certain action, adopt certain values, or otherwise conform in order to be accepted."

You could have probably given me that same definition since most people know what peer pressure means. The thing about it I don't understand is why it is only ever talked about as a bad thing. Don't get me wrong, it can be a really bad thing. Examples of the undeniably negative results of peer pressure would be: your group of friends are bullying someone and they want you to join in, and it makes you feel awful but you do it to fit in; your friends convince you to use drugs when you wouldn't otherwise for fear of negative consequences; or when your friends convince you to spend a night out when you know your time would be better spent studying or resting for your next work shift or class, but you go along against your better judgment.

However, peers can be positive influencers as well. I would not have joined my high school tennis or basketball teams if two other girls who joined hadn't suggested I do the same. Tennis is still one of my great loves, and I'd be missing out if Lisa hadn't suggested I try out for the team.

In Larry Winget's book *You're Broke Because You Want To Be*, he says your income is typically the average of your five closest friends. Many successful people have proposed the average five concept relates to more areas of our lives than finances. Your fitness level, your happiness, your career success can also be figured based on your five closest friends. The word 'friend' is vague. In most cases, it refers to the people with whom you spend most of your time.

I'd like to think I made good choices in life because I was born with the skill to envision a brighter future for myself. However, I am smart enough to know that my friend Lisa had a huge impact on me. We spent a lot of time together. I was blessed with a best friend who had no desire for trouble, which kept me from having to make hard decisions constantly. My brother chose a crowd overwhelmed by the temptation for whatever was fast, easy, and rebellious. He was a quick learner and a talented manipulator, so I can't say whether a better crowd would have kept him from misbehaving or not, but it certainly would have challenged his judgment more often.

Changing Peer Groups

Your life map changes as you age and learn. It's a small percentage of people whose career plans in high school go unchanged as they get older. Most of us learn new things, find paths we didn't know existed, and meet people who open our minds to topics we hadn't considered before. It's natural, even necessary sometimes, for us to alter our plans. I bet you can relate. Maybe you have changed your mind many times regarding what kind of career you'd like to have.

Think of a time when you started a new job, changed an academic focus, or joined a new group. Even dating someone new can open up a whole new peer group when you meet his or her friends. As the design of our lives change, the people with whom we spend the majority of our time shifts concurrently. If you have people in your life who mean a lot to you, but aren't accommodating to your goals, it doesn't mean you have to cut them out of your life, but it may mean you spend the majority of your time with people who do align with your goals. It is important to understand this concept.

The people you spend the majority of your time with will have an impact on your outcomes.

To put this principle to use, you may decide you need to find some new people to add to your circle of five. You're probably not going to go up to someone who is succeeding in an area you strive for and ask, "Would you like to be my friend and hang out?"

A plan is more likely to prosper if it puts you in a situation in which they get to know you naturally. Here are some examples to consider. If you have an associate or classmate you'd like to get to know better, you could invite him or her to lunch. Another idea is you could host a small gathering with the purpose of networking. Provide snacks, drinks and venue and send invitations to those you'd like to attend. Create the opportunity to chat with them. You could join or start an extra-curricular group at school and invite them to join too. You could volunteer or take a part-time position with a company in order to establish a connection. You could create a mastermind group or study group they'll also benefit from and invite them to join.

How Positive Peer Relationships Impacted My Success

When I was 19-years-old, and in college, I would make the two-hour drive home to work on the weekends and also to see Lisa. She, her older brother, and one of his friends became my closest group of friends from my hometown. They were avid skiers. They would water ski in the summer and snow ski in the winter. I went on the slopes with them a couple of times, but being new to the sport, I wasn't very good.

One snowy weekend, I came home from college, and they had a surprise for me. They had bought me a pair of snow skis. They all chipped in, because they knew I didn't have extra money to spend. I was paying for college, and renting skis again and again would get expensive. They said it was an early Christmas present.

I'm sure they were expecting a grand reaction for such a grand gesture, and when they didn't get one, they were disappointed. That was the most expensive gift anyone had ever given me, and all I could think of was how they spent a lot of money on something I wasn't good at and didn't love the way they did.

The next day, we headed to the ski resort where I'd get to use my new skis. They would speed by with big smiles on their faces, cut hard at the bottom of the hill spraying snow and stopping seemingly effortlessly, and I would throw myself on the ground because that was the only way I knew how to stop. Any time I wanted to give up or sit one out, they'd tell me, "It just takes practice. Everyone struggles at first, but you keep doing it and you get better. If you quit, you'll never improve."

Not wanting to be the loser whose friends gave her an expensive gift only to waste it by not using it, I kept at it. And I'm glad I did, because some of my fondest memories are skiing with those guys. I did get better. I became stable, could keep up with them going down the run, and learned to stop at the bottom without bruising my bottom. I spent my winter on those skis and the next summer on a wakeboard, which also had a learning curve I had to conquer.

That group of young adults taught me a valuable insight. If I hadn't learned to keep going when things got rough, I may have learned instead that difficulty was a sign of being on the wrong path, a reason to quit and do something different. If they hadn't convinced me, I probably would have thought skiing just wasn't for me and moved on. That lesson has impacted my life many times since. Everyone needs to know it, because everyone fails. Using failure as a platform for growth rather than a sign of a dead-end is how to create a life of accomplishments. I'm lucky to have learned that from my peers.

That wasn't the only experience I had with helpful peers. As each semester of college got going, I paid attention to which classmates were performing well and sat next to them so I'd have a higher chance of striking up a conversation and forming quality study groups. In my first sales job, I would arrive to team meetings early or stay late to talk with the representatives turning in the best sales numbers in the hopes of learning from them.

Each time I was in a new situation or position, I would find the people with the most influence or the best records and earn their time and attention. They'd become part of my circle. I'd learn from them, offer to help when they needed it, and fashion a mutually beneficial relationship. I'm making it sound formal, but in most cases it was as simple as making an effort to be likeable and helpful. Over the past fifteen years, the majority of my personal and professional growth can be attributed to the people with whom I worked or spent time.

Each of those people had their own strengths. Some were in fabulously successful marriages, some were living lives of superb health and fitness, some were financial virtuosos, some were authorities in leadership, some were specialists in building lasting relationships, and some were inspiring communicators. I have improved in every one of those areas in my own life because of what I learned from those individuals. Without them, I wouldn't be the person I am now.

Julian's Story—Negative Peers Hurt and Positive Peers Help

Julian is a young man I met when he was part of a group of young professionals I was working with—a mastermind group I was coordinating. He is a good example of someone whose peer group affected his performance in a very negative manner.

Before his junior year of high school, Julian started hanging out with a new group of friends. Most of the time, they would get together to smoke pot. For six months of his senior year of high school, Julian got into a lot of trouble. He was on probation at school, failed drug tests, got arrested for fighting and for drugs, was kicked out of school, assigned to an outpatient rehab program, and he was also fighting a lot with his family. He only made it halfway through rehab before he started using drugs again. He did make one improvement, but it was an increase in the skill of using tricks to pass the urine tests.

Julian said, "Once I was arrested, I was on the cops' radar. Even during the times I wasn't doing anything wrong, I would suffer police harassment. One day, while sitting in front of my house, not breaking laws of any kind, the cops showed up. They treated me like a criminal in front of my neighbors. That was a low point for me."

Julian didn't have any direction. He talked about times when he'd try to get back on the right path and the changes seemed impossible. He'd make an effort to get better but he'd end up in more trouble somehow, and he was having run-ins with the cops more often. Soon after, he was ticketed as a Minor In Possession of alcohol and was caught stealing pizza. "My circle of influence was really bad," Julian said, "and I couldn't figure out what to do."

At that same time, he really liked a girl whose dad happened to work in the police department. Of course, her dad didn't want her spending any time with Julian. In fact, he said there was no chance Julian could date his daughter. Julian knew he'd have to be better if he was going to change her dad's mind.

In an unusual twist of events, while Julian was out drinking in New Orleans one evening, around 3AM he ran into a fortune-teller, and she gave him a free reading. Overall, she gave him a positive view of his future. Whether or not you believe in her ability to actually tell the future is irrelevant. What is important is she was the first person, in a while, to tell him convincingly he could have a better life than what he currently had.

From then on, he started making positive changes. The most important of those changes was he distanced himself from his negative peer group. He even sacrificed the semester trip in order to keep that distance. He started a new job and gained a whole new peer group of more positive people his age. He really liked it and worked hard to succeed. It gave him a sense of direction he didn't have before.

Today, Julian is 22-years-old and no longer taking part in criminal activity. He says he is exactly where he wants to be. He's in a great job, earning more than $75,000 a year and he's able to give back by coaching others at his company. He also feels like he's able to be a positive influence on his younger brother who looks up to him. Julian is living his dream, has the freedom to travel, and his parents are proud of him. He recently graduated from college and is debt free with more than $20,000 saved. That is an exciting accomplishment not many college graduates can claim these days.

Vehicles to Take You to AWESOME

Evaluate your current peer group. Do they influence you in positive or negative ways? If it's negative, it would be beneficial for you to find other peers that could impact you more positively.

Evaluate what you bring to the group. Do you need to make any changes for the benefit of your peers?

Seek people to add to your peer group who could benefit from it and bring benefit to it. A solid first step is just keeping your eyes and mind open to the idea when meeting people. You'll begin to notice people with whom you'd like to spend more time.

Joining groups is a great way to meet new people. You can find groups based on interests you already have. When I moved to Austin, TX, I joined a Meetup.com group for tennis. Meetup.com has diverse groups all over the nation. Also, college campuses have a multitude of groups—business, hobby, athletic, and school sponsored. There are also youth, community, nonprofit, and church organizations that have groups that can be joined. Finding a group is the easy part. Having the courage to join a new group is where your determination will be demonstrated.

Now that we've talked about how your peers can have a positive or negative impact on you, let's look at how your effect on others impacts you. You'd be missing pieces of the puzzle if you thought your actions toward other people only affects other people. You'll read about both negative and positive examples of mine in the next chapter.

Gone In 600 Seconds

Brainstorm two lists: The ways your peers affect you positively and the ways your peers affect you negatively. For ideas on how peers can affect you, visit http:// amieemueller.com/peer-pressure-or-peer-power/

Which list is longer? If the negative list is longer, consider cutting back on the time spent with them. Then make a list of qualities you'd like to have in a beneficial peer group. This understanding is the first step in finding new, positive peers.

If the positive list is longer, that is great news. You can still think of ways to help each other get to an even higher level of support and accomplishment. A great idea is to discuss it with them and have them help you brainstorm.

Look for other brainstorm exercises in the *Destination Awesome Action Guide* at the back of the book.

Chapter 5

HOW YOU AFFECT OTHERS AFFECTS YOU

an you think of a time when you helped someone? Hurt someone? How did each of those make you feel?

Whether our impact on others is intentional or not, we feel the intrinsic consequences. Do you have any notes of gratitude—others thanking you for your impact on them? Those notes are some of my most treasured possessions. Why are those personal notes one of the keepsakes we hold on to and what makes them special to us?

While at a Tony Robbins leadership training event a few years ago, I received a piece of unexpected and brilliant advice. I went to the event looking for ways to improve one of my self-determined weaknesses, and one of the leaders suggested I focus on the impact I have on those I help rather than improving that particular skill in myself. In doing so, their belief was my weakness would no longer have much bearing. It was a perspective I hadn't considered but made sense when someone else pointed it out.

Let me take you back to a time when my impact on others wasn't so positive so I can show you why it's important to be aware of your effect on people.

Since my dad's work as a nationwide truck driver kept him away from home, one of his major challenges was finding someone to be with my brother and me. The main concern was just satisfying the legal requirements of us not being alone so the state wouldn't take us from him. There was a time when my dad gave up on the constant turnover of low-quality babysitters and asked his younger sister (my aunt Mary) to move in with us. She was a single mother so she agreed, and she and my two-year-old cousin, Brian, made our trailer their mailing address. Mary needed some help at the time also, so it should have been a win-win. It probably would have worked out great if the baggage my brother and I carried hadn't already been so heavy.

I was 9-years-old at the time, and as hard as I try, there isn't much I remember about living with her or my cousin. When I concentrate, I come up with snapshots: falling out of a tree and Mary picking thorns out of my back from the pointy bush I landed in and Mary crying after a heated confrontation with my brother. She didn't stay with us long. Shortly after a nervous breakdown, Mary moved out. The occurrence I remember most from her time with us, though I wish I could forget, was related to my impact on Brian. And when I say impact, boy do I mean impact!

Mary had to work to support herself and her son, so while she worked, I became the free babysitter. Looking back, I'm not sure she got her money's worth. It's not that I had a mean streak. I never have. However, I did have a short temper.

In our home, spankings were implemented from time to time. I'm not sure how it began, but the wooden spoon was the tool of choice. For as long as I can remember, it was related more to whippings than cooking, though it was used for both. It had a handle about a foot long, a small oval face, and was the color of raw, unfinished maple. Maple may be one of the best woods for cooking utensils due to its non-toxic qualities, but it was not a utensil I loved.

So one day when Brian was being an ornery 2-year-old (is there any other kind?), I hit my boiling point quickly. To this day, I don't remember what Brian did exactly. I just know I grabbed the wooden spoon to spank his bottom just like I had learned was appropriate for persuading unruly kids. He was still in diapers at the time, which I figured was like having a butt cushion, so I believed it was more about instilling fear than hurting him. However, things don't always go the way you think they will.

With Brian's left arm in my left hand and the wooden punisher in my right, I took a back swing that would make any golf coach proud. A second before I connected with his diaper, he bent his knees and fell to the floor. Unintentionally, the spoon connected with skin on his lower back. It only took one hit to send him into a screaming fit and to leave a red mark that lasted for days. Aunt Mary noticed the mark when she returned from work that evening and broke down into tears, yet again.

Linda Elder of the Critical Thinking Community at CriticalThinking.org has a practical theory of the mind that states there are a minimum of three basic functions in the brain: cognitive, emotional, and volition or will. So even though the thinking part of my brain tells the feeling part of my brain that I was only 9 and shouldn't be too hard on myself for mistakes made at that age, the emotional part rebuts with a strong argument of guilty feelings. The lesson I learned was this: though I've done many things to myself that were not good for my own body or mind, none of them has as strong of a grip on me as the memory of hurting someone else.

An Insult for the Greater Good

On the opposite side, we can take comfort in knowing that same principle holds true for memories of helping another. My senior year of high school, after twelve years of being intentionally quiet to avoid ridicule, I did something out of character that not only shocked me and those around me, but ended with my only-ever detention.

There was a girl in my speech class cursed with a little more facial hair than average. She was one of those teenage girls with dark hair, and it was starting to come in on her upper lip as well. In that same class was a boy who enjoyed picking on people. On this particular day, she was unlucky enough to be the target of his bullying. So after witnessing him pick on her about hair on her face for about ten minutes and her sitting quietly with no comebacks, I had one of those moments we all dream of—a clever quip that came to me in the moment rather than five minutes after its window of opportunity.

I turned to him and said quite loudly, "You're just mad that she has more hair on her face than you have on your balls!" It was so unexpected the whole room was silent for a beat followed by a roaring laughter. I think I heard it for the first time when everyone else did. It popped into my brain and out of my mouth before I really processed it. The noise died quickly as we realized the teacher had walked into the room a nanosecond before the words passed over my lips. It was one of those TV moments where you say something inappropriate only to find out the adult is standing right behind you. I did the slow turn and found the teacher in the spot that would have made any sitcom director proud.

I know I shouldn't be admitting this because I broke school rules, got myself into trouble, and used language that was inappropriate in school, but it was all totally worth it just to see the look on the bully's face as well as the expression on the girl's face when someone stood up for her. If she felt as if she wasn't alone even for a moment, it was worth it. As far as I know, he never ridiculed her on the subject again. I feel good about standing up for her that day, and just as hurting others sticks with us, so do the times we help others.

Since then, I've focused on helping others in more positive ways including being kind, opening doors for strangers, volunteering for community organizations, donating to multiple charities, and letting the occasional shopper with fewer items cut in front of me in the checkout line. Nothing is too big or too small if it makes a positive impact on someone else. It will also benefit you even if only for the intrinsic value it brings to your sense of contribution and self-worth.

Ryan's Story—From Frustrated to Fulfilled

One of my good friends and former colleague, Ryan, showed up to his twentieth birthday frustrated and fed up. When he graduated high school, his biggest fear was getting caught up in the rat race—no matter how hard you work or spin the wheel, you never get ahead. He felt like he was being consumed and was wearing out after years of working in construction, as a mechanic, and in other manual labor jobs.

"I was bitter from running into dead ends," Ryan said. "I was fed up with my circumstances, but even more frustrating was I kept seeing people who had the wealth I wanted but they weren't happy. They were abusing substances or just generally discontent." Ryan wanted financial success, but even more than that, he wanted happiness and fulfillment. And all were eluding him.

Soon after, he started a new job as an aircraft mechanic, which is where he met Cliff. Regarding Cliff, Ryan said, "I really looked up to him. He was just a little older than me, he was flying around the world to negotiate transactions for the company, the guys liked him, the girls loved him, he drove a hot car—a Corvette—and he made me feel appreciated. He made everyone feel that way." When Cliff invited Ryan to join him for a concert in Austin, Texas, though Ryan wasn't a fan of the band, he accepted without question.

When the show wrapped up, Ryan and Cliff headed to the infamous Sixth Street in downtown Austin. It is an area of the city lined with clubs, bars, and restaurants. It gets so busy with foot traffic, the officials put up barriers to block off the road so cars cannot get through. Sixth Street is basically one big party, and with University of Texas only a few blocks away, the majority of partygoers are young adults. Ryan was more than ready. This was going to be his first chance to use his fake ID in what felt like an exclusive place.

It was around eleven in the evening and the foot traffic had just started to pick up. Ryan and Cliff walked by many clubs and a homeless guy sitting on the sidewalk while they checked out the scene. A little farther up the road, they came to a pizza place with an order window right on the street. Cliff stopped and ordered some beer and pizza and walked back to where the homeless guy was sitting. Ryan followed.

The two men sat down and started chatting with the vagrant who was initially taken aback. It was clear he was not expecting anyone to stop. Cliff offered him some of their food and drink, which the man happily accepted. "We sat there for just under an hour," Ryan said. "We shared stories and dinner like you would with any friend." As they sat there, everyone else on Sixth Street walked on by.

Ryan said, "The homeless guy expressed gratitude many times while we sat with him. Cliff treated him the same way he treated everyone else—with kindness and respect. That night brought me back to something I had forgotten or I had gotten distracted from: it's important to see the good in others and have a love for everyone." Ryan describes that night as a reminder he didn't have to go through life with blinders on, with a cage around his heart or just pushing through it. It gave him a new energy and a new perspective.

Ryan is now in his early 30's. He is a successful entrepreneur and is involved in many successful ventures. About his proudest accomplishment he says, "I used to produce out of fear and now I produce out of love." He works hard to make sure his office is a good environment for his employees and customers. "They can tell we are genuine. We take the time to help our customers understand our products and services and the value it provides them." Ryan lives in his dream area on a beautiful island. He is debt free, has the finances to do what he wants and feels he is building something that gives him the time to enjoy his life.

On helping others, Ryan said, "You can't say something negative to others without feeling those negative emotions yourself, and who you are speaks louder than your words anyway."

In short, helping others helps you, and helping yourself be happier helps others too.

Vehicles to Take You to
AWESOME

Find ways to have a positive impact on others each day. For a list of conscious acts of kindness, visit http://amieemueller.com/intentional-acts-of-kindness. Leave a comment if you'd like to add something to the list. I'd love to hear from you and see the list grow.

Avoid hurting others, because as you do, it's a detriment to you as well.

Forgive yourself and earn forgiveness from others. If you've hurt others in the past, you can't change it, but you can attempt to make up for it. In Shawn Achor's book *The Happiness Advantage*, he explains the results of a decade of research by psychologist and business consultant Marcial Losada. In short, "It takes about three positive comments, experiences, or expressions to fend off the languishing effects of one negative." To me that means if you want to create happiness, make sure you perform a minimum of three positive acts for every negative one. If you've hurt the same person twenty times, make the decision to make it up to them by completing sixty or more affirmative deeds at least equal in size to what you want to absolve. Also, do your best to not perform more negative acts. Maybe you're thinking, "Yeah right, weirdo. It can't be that simple."

But it can be.

If you choose an existence of bringing positivity to the world, your world will be more positive. After all, it's all the same world. You can't make it better for others without making it better for yourself.

Gone In 600 Seconds

Check out the list of acts of kindness at http://amieemueller.com/intentional-acts-of-kindness and choose seven of them you'd like to do. Do one each day for seven days, or do all seven in one day. When you've finished all seven acts of kindness, send me a message or a video and let me know how it impacted you. You can go to my message page http://amieemueller.com/contact/. I'd love to hear from you and maybe I'll post it on my site.

BE SUPPORTIVE AND OPEN TO LEARNING FROM OTHERS

Chapter 6

When I was 16-years-old, I was a passenger in a car being driven by a high school friend named Barb who was a year older than me and a new driver. We were heading from my place to her parents' home, which took us on a route that included many country roads. Most of the scenery was farmland and forest. It was common for the animals in the area such as deer, squirrels, raccoons, cats, and groundhogs, to run into the roads. Over the years, my car was the unintended reaper for the deaths of so many small animals, I'm surprised I don't have nightmares of PETA's revenge.

On this particular trip, Barb and I were on a narrow road cutting through a wooded area when our day took a stressful turn. The engine started to rev and Barb began freaking out. She exclaimed, "The pedal is stuck!"

The accelerator pedal had molded itself to the car floor and would not release. Barb's response to the dilemma was to let go of the steering wheel and use her hands to cover her face while exclaiming a series of "Oh my Gods." I grabbed the wheel and sternly said her name to grab her attention. "Put your hands back on the wheel!" I said, and she did. "No matter what, always hold on to the wheel."

From there, the car continued to rev higher and higher, and I started throwing out ideas. Stomping on the gas pedal didn't work. Riding the breaks was a bad idea, because the rpms (that other big gauge in the dashboard, next to the miles per hour) kept getting higher, which wasn't good for the engine or the brakes. My last idea was to shift from drive into neutral. The engine screamed as it was still being overloaded with fuel while in neutral, so she immediately popped it back into drive. Something gave when she did, and the pedal released. The car began to decelerate.

Once we had it stopped on the side of the road, we looked at each other and broke into laughter. It was a joy filled with relief. We drove slowly from there to her house, never pushing the gas pedal very far, and continued with our plans for the day.

In a vehicle, do you like to be the driver or a passenger? Each one has a role in both transportation and in life.

By the time I was 18-years-old, I had been in seven car accidents. Only one of those was as a driver for which I made a last-minute decision to turn right out of the left lane, not seeing the car in my blind spot that would ram into me as I cut into their driving space. As a passenger on icy roads, I've experienced carving donuts through people's yards, slamming into a parked truck, running into a jackknifed semi trailer, being rear ended by a woman driving on snow for the first time, and sliding into snow drifts. I've also had the pleasure of hydroplaning off a country road into a muddy cornfield during a rainstorm. A tow truck was needed to pull the car out of that mess. It's not surprising I've had vertebrae alignment issues and many trips to the chiropractor.

For me, being a passenger is more challenging than being a driver. I think it is because I have to relinquish control to the person behind the steering wheel. If you've ever dealt with a side-seat driver, you've probably shared a car with someone who isn't excited to surrender that power either. In most cases, if the passenger feels safe with the driver, usually meaning they are confident in both their knowledge of directions and driving habits, not a lot of debate occurs in the vehicle. When the passenger is under the impression they could do it better or safer, it often leads to debate, usually while in the car together.

Here's the deal we all make when getting into a vehicle: drivers need to be worthy of the trust people put in them, and passengers need to accept they are not in control—a power they relinquish when they get in, close the door, and buckle up. On a side note, never get in a vehicle with a driver too impaired, distracted, or careless to have your safety as a priority.

Control Versus Support

As is true when you are a car passenger, there are times in life when it is necessary to let someone else be in the lead or have control of a situation. To help others along their own journeys, sometimes we have to let them take the lead and only offer our advice when it is requested. It is also important to remember to support them and help them succeed. Solving the stuck accelerator issue had a direct impact on me since I was in the car. However, let's say it had only been Barb in the car and she called me for help during the event. I would have still felt a sense of urgency to help her figure it out, because she is my friend and I want her to be happy and safe.

The times it is probably most difficult to be supportive of others is when you are in direct competition with them or you feel they are not doing things as well as you would if you were in control. Have you ever been overlooked when a leadership role was decided? You may have had a fleeting moment of weakness, relishing in the idea of the chosen one's failure and the scrap we're given when we get to say, "I told you so." We've all probably had a similar thought a time or two. It is not an empowering thought for ourselves or a supportive thought for those around us, and it is up to us to fight that mindset.

Even if you are the one in a position to decide who gets to lead, unsupportive thoughts may still try to creep into your mind. You don't need to punish yourself for having those thoughts. Just recognize it, let it pass, and don't act on it. In other words, rise above it.

The purpose of letting someone else lead isn't so they will fall and we can step in with an "I told you I should have been in charge from the beginning." We build a stronger self, inner circle, network, and society when we help each other achieve. When Barb lost it temporarily and let go of the wheel, I didn't take the opportunity to criticize her driving skills, yell at her, or give up completely and wait for whatever outcome would play out. I convinced her to get back on track, threw out some ideas, and stayed as calm as I could in the midst of the crisis. We both look back at that day with humor. Had I reacted poorly, it would be a regretful memory.

There are times you are being cheered on by your loved ones, and there are times when your role is to be the cheerleader. Since we know our effect on others has an impact on us too, it makes being a supportive friend, co-worker, or family member important for both parties' sakes.

Patton's Story—Losing to His Competition and Gaining Valuable Insight

One of my good friends and colleagues, Patton Sides, was always a high achiever. He grew up in a good family with a loving mother and father. His dad was an accountant and his mom was a social worker. Patton was a high performing student at Abilene High School, a participant in theater and an athlete in both football and power lifting, a state qualifier in the latter. During his sophomore year of high school, the students were told where they currently ranked in the class and the top two at graduation would be allowed to give speeches. From that moment on, Patton's main goal was to give a speech at graduation, which was little more than two years away.

Patton made a lot of sacrifices to put himself on the path to valedictorian. He missed social events and he worked very hard in class and on assignments. He put his full effort into every paper and every test.

One month before graduation, he was called into the principal's office and told he was currently the top student in the class. He would need to start preparing his speech. Patton was ecstatic. Two weeks later, however, they called him back in to say they had miscalculated and he was actually not number one. Patton was okay with that because number two gets to speak as well. The principal told him he was not number two either. He was actually number three, and he would not be giving a speech. Patton was devastated. When he thought about the two years of sacrifices and hard work he put in to be in the top two, his heart ached.

Prior to the ceremony itself, the school held a news conference recognizing the top twenty-five in the class. They also gave special recognition to the valedictorian and salutatorian. The kids sat in order of their class rank, so Patton was sitting next to the top two students when his dad arrived. His dad, knowing how much Patton wanted to be in the top two, headed over to where he was sitting, walked straight to the top two kids and said, "I'm Patton's father, Mr. Sides, and I just wanted to tell you that I'm proud of you. Congratulations for earning the top two spots in the class."

Patton describes that day as, "A lesson in life that it's important to always be happy for other people's successes. I also realized that my results aren't the only things that define me. My response to those results is as much or more important."

The school decided to make an exception to the rules, in light of the miscalculation, and allowed three students to give speeches that year. Patton would give his speech after all.

Turns out, that day wasn't special because of the message Patton gave but because of the message he received.

Patton is still a high achiever. He double majored in college and graduated with honors and a 3.72 GPA. His first job after college was as a high school teacher and coach. He coached pole vaulting athletes and football players. Patton recollects many times when that same lesson came in handy, especially when his team or his athletes would underperform and concede victory. Patton said, "You always wanted your kids to win, but when they didn't, you were still happy for the other kids and their coaches. We were still a community, and we all had the same goals and intentions for our students, so it made sense to be supportive of each other in spite of the competition."

He went on to earn a masters degree for which his thesis was nominated for an award, and now he is a successful entrepreneur and coordinator of a small team of sales representatives in the Lone Star Division of Vector Marketing, who produce more than half a million in sales each year in just the program he manages. Each year, his team is in the top five in the company's competition of more than 50 teams.

When his sales team is working an event together, their sales combine for a team competitive total, but each rep also gets personal commissions for their particular sales. Since sales have their ups and downs, there are times when

Patton's teammates are having more success than he is, and there is always a slight twinge of competitiveness to overcome.

Patton said, "I've found that being happy for their success, even when I'm challenged with lower sales, makes a difference in my results. By maintaining a positive outlook and supportive attitude, I have turned some bad days around which otherwise would have ended poorly. Even on the days when my results aren't great, I find setting that example teaches the rest of my team to support each other's successes, which leads to a happier team overall."

Build Your Skills by Sharing with Others

Being supportive of others had a huge impact on my business as well. For six years, I was a recruiter and sales team developer. I worked with more than a thousand sales representatives during that time. We represented a product that was also represented by many other sales teams in the nation. The other managers and I utilized the same training program for new reps and shared ideas with each other on making our groups highly successful. We held conferences a few times a year for which all of the reps and sales managers would come together for advanced training. My team built a reputation that led to other managers asking how to develop something similar in their offices, which led to my speaking and helping train hundreds of business owners within that direct sales community.

My sales team became known for being a tight-knit group with a high level of support and respect for each other. We were also acknowledged for being professional, ethical, and having good rep retention. Our team had a lot of fun together and was consistently in the top 15% of sales nationally. There is one record we still hold to this day and it pertains to the level of help our team members provided each other.

There is a philosophy I shared with my sales reps during their first week and continued to share as a reminder many times throughout their careers. I believe in this philosophy as it relates to business, health, relationships, financial success, and any other skill one wants to develop.

The keys to this philosophy are:

- Each person has something positive to share no matter who they are, what his experience, or where she comes from.
- To become worthy of success in any area, it is necessary to learn the skills needed to achieve it.
- The way to get those skills is to seek the strengths in others and learn from them in exchange for teaching them your strength.

Let's say there are twenty characteristics that guarantee your success in whatever endeavor you seek to achieve. In other words, if you have these twenty things, you'll be successful. They could be traits like confidence, time management skills, discipline, a sense of humor, and trustworthiness.

In addition, each person has at least one of these characteristics. After all, we each have strengths and weaknesses. The way for you to get more of the twenty is to work with someone else and each share your strength with the other. Once you've done that, and mastered it, you each now have two of the twenty characteristics. Then you both find a third teammate and share each of your strengths, and once mastered, you all now have three of the twenty. And so on. The way to get all twenty positive traits for success is to learn from everyone you work with what their strengths are and share your skills with each other. This can apply to everyone you meet, volunteer with, go to church with, are classmates with and so on.

In the end, we had a group of people looking for the good in others, working together, supporting each other, and learning from each other in order to reach their goals. When that principle took shape within our team and continued to reproduce itself without needing my instigating, it became a culture for which I was grateful and proud. To this day, that supportive and team-oriented culture is what I miss the most when I think of my time with them.

I've found there are also times you will see good in others they do not see in themselves. Sometimes, you will believe in others after they have given up on themselves. A great example is Norman Vincent Peale. After Norman wrote his first book, he sought publishing. Being rejected many times, the frustrated writer threw his manuscript in the trash. His wife pulled it out of the garbage and sent it to one last publisher. That simple act of believing in him and supporting his goal, even without his knowledge and beyond his own perseverance, made all of the difference.

Norman Vincent Peale is the author of *The Power of Positive Thinking*, which was on the New York Time's Bestseller list for 186 weeks in a row and has sold more than five million copies. Had she not done that for her husband, Mr. Peale wouldn't have been the only one it affected. More than five million readers would have missed out on a great book.

What would we find in your garbage? Something the world needs or wants? Something that could change lives, even if only the lives of your family, neighbors, or friends? I invite you to share with our community what you would love to share with the world by posting it on our Facebook page. Simply type, "I want to share with the world..." and then let us know what it is. Find the page by searching Amiee Mueller – Destination Awesome.

Look for the good in everyone you meet. It's there. Sometimes you have to dig a little deeper, but if you search for it, you will find it. Everyone has positive aspects.

The kid hooked on drugs and skipping school may be one of the best drummers you'll ever meet, which was the case with my brother. The timid kid who never speaks in class may be the best student in school. The mother that appears to be neglecting her child may be doing so because she cares greatly for the welfare of her kids and believes they are better off without her. Some of the seemingly worst behaviors aren't evidence of people's worthlessness. It may mean they haven't yet found a way to make their strengths evident.

Be open to learning from others. Sometimes we learn things we didn't know we needed. Every person knows something we don't, and we know something they don't. Both parties being open to learning from each other is most beneficial. If someone doesn't have a strength you are currently seeking, it just means they can probably teach you something else you hadn't thought to learn.

Support others on their paths to success. Helping others achieve their goals doesn't make you look bad in comparison to their achievement. Rather, it solidifies your position as an important and respected piece of their network; it strengthens your role in their lives. Who will they turn to the next time they want a trusted ally, helpful advice, or to bestow appreciation? Most likely, they'll turn to the people who helped them succeed.

Selecting beneficial peers, increasing the positivity you put into the world while decreasing the negativity, and supporting others on their paths to fulfillment are all things you can do now. In fact, you are doing it now. By reading this book, you are engaging in positive thoughts and supporting me in my goal to help others choose progress and achieve it.

The reason you can start now is because they are all simply choices you make. There are already people in your life. You are making empowering choices by deciding to be supportive of their goals, be mindful of your influence on them, and evaluate how much of your time you want to give to them.

We've laid the asphalt on the Road Paved in Relationships, and now it's time to talk about the final step: painting the lines that will keep you heading straight toward your awesome destination. The next chapter talks about one of the most important strategies of successful people all over the world, and I'll share with you how simple it is to implement into your own plan.

Gone In 600 Seconds

Make a list of the five to ten people closest to you. Next to each person's name, write out one to three strengths they possess. Do you also have those strengths? If not, set your intention to learn from them how to improve in those areas.

For more exercises to help you cultivate healthy and beneficial relationships with your peers and others, turn to the *Destination Awesome Action Guide* at the back of the book.

A MENTOR IS THE HUMAN VERSION OF GOOGLE SEARCH

Chapter 7

How many times a day do you search something on the web? For me, it's anywhere from one to twenty, depending on what's going on that day. Can you imagine a world without the web search function? It's hard to even consider, isn't it? Good for us Google isn't going anywhere. Whew!

You are competent and practiced in Google search, but have you utilized the human version of Google yet? It is another resource not to be underestimated. It is absolutely constructive and abundantly available, yet not as common of a practice as it should be. Mentorship is its name, and providing answers for success, in any area of life, is its game. I've experienced the undeniable benefits of having a mentor.

A Lesson in Bad Mentoring

It was late, and I was watching TV—my usual evening activity when I was 8-years-old. My dad and his friend rushed in through the trailer door carrying a big, black trash bag that appeared to be full. They were excited and hurried through the TV room to his bedroom in the back. A couple of days later, while

I was walking out of my babysitter's trailer, I saw a gallon sized plastic bag full of green plant handed to her.

Pot in exchange for childcare. Yup. That happened. When a marijuana patch was discovered in a cornfield, who knew it would lead to a means of paying the babysitter? Apparently there is more than one kind of green people will accept as payment for watching kids. I think that classifies as an act performed by adults, who were supposed to be my role models, that was less than ideal for me to witness.

Both of my parents remarried, so I have four when you count step-parents. One of my parents was an alcoholic, one was high a lot of the time, one was away most of the time working, and the last was just away most of the time. My older brother spent most of his life in and out of detention centers, jails, and prisons and in and out of reality, since he used drugs the majority of a 12-year span. Looking back, it's clear to me I didn't have positive role models in my home environment. It's not surprising I excelled academically, because school was my safe place and teachers were the people I looked up to.

Again, the people in my family weren't all bad. I wasn't physically beaten or on the street. They sent me to school where I was fed and put on a path that would lead to my liberation from my childhood conditions. However, there were times I wore the same clothes for days, was left to devise my own meals which usually meant Spaghetti O's, PB&Js, cereal or mac and cheese, and many instances I was seeing things at such a young age it would make the Motion Picture Association of America film rating team cringe.

I saw my first pornographic film when I was 10. That was before the Internet made it widely accessible and difficult to police. I witnessed people do drugs at that same age. I watched people curse and scream at each other almost weekly. I read fewer than ten books my entire childhood outside of schoolwork, and don't recall witnessing those around me with their noses in books either.

When my brother hit 12-years-old, his libido kicked in. After that, not many of our babysitters resisted his wiles, as most ended up in his bed while I watched TV. I'm not sure if that speaks more to the lack of quality in our caregivers or the exceptional persuasiveness of my brother. Overall, my parents made many bad choices as young adults and disqualified themselves as positive mentors, which left me socially inadequate and ignorant in the ways of successful people.

My Experience With Positive Mentors

My teachers in the Lakeland School District from kindergarten through twelfth grade were fine examples. I didn't know anything of their personal lives, but I could see their passion for their work, the accountability they required, the behavior they tolerated or didn't, and the manner of their communication. They didn't scream or curse at anyone, they looked professional and they were there every day. They showed up. Teachers were the most consistent role models in my childhood, and from them, I learned the basics of how ones supposed to behave in a professional environment.

Early in my sophomore year of college, I was fortunate to find a sales job that would lead to my meeting many quality individuals who became my mentors. As I moved up in the organization, I'd meet and begin learning from new people. That became my pattern in any position. After fifteen years, I was basically a new, thriving person. I started as an angry, untrusting, unconfident, poor communicator. Less than two decades later, I spent most of my time coaching sales reps and business owners and planning events in which they'd get the opportunity to learn. Even after my massive growth, as I mentor others, I still have mentors for myself. Learning from others had the largest impact on my development.

Chuck's Story—A Move from Meaningless to Meaningful

One of the best examples I can share of the impact of mentoring is the story of my friend Chuck, a business owner where I'm also a customer. By age sixteen, Chuck had already spent years earning bad grades, hanging out with a troublesome group of kids, and suffering from an abusive and alcoholic mother. His junior year of high school, while other students were buzzing about the SAT test and college coming soon, Chuck was skipping school, doing drugs, and mostly agreeing with his teachers who labeled him as a kid with no future who was mostly worthless. The friend he looked up to the most was a guy with the skill to hide his drug use from his affluent parents so he could still reap the monetary benefits of their trust.

Chuck didn't have any future in mind for himself and didn't care. The decisions he was making about his future went as far as the next hour or so. Would he go to class next period and where would he take his next hit? He used drugs five to seven times a day, and for six months, he was high 24/7. In his mind, consequences meant nothing.

After an arrest for possession, he could no longer hide his drug habit from his family, something he had been doing well up to that point. Rather than deal with a volatile environment at his mom's house, and to inflict as much pain on her as he could imagine, he decided to leave her and see if his biological father would take him in. His dad and step-mom moved Chuck into their home without hesitation, and for the first time, Chuck experienced something new: a heart-to-heart conversation involving no apparent disappointment or yelling. His step-mom was the one who came to him for that conversation. Chuck said, "She was the first person to take a genuine interest in me without judgment." That was the beginning of Chuck's turning point.

After the judge assigned to his drug arrest suggested he go to rehab, Chuck's dad drove him to the rehab facility. Chuck initially went through the motions just to satisfy his dad and the court, meanwhile rolling around ideas of how he was going to get out of it. Weeks later, he came to realize rehab was what he wanted. He spent nearly five months in the program. He did so well there, he became a mentor to new guys. He excelled and the center offered him a job. Chuck said, "It felt rewarding to help others. Dedicating time to helping others was what made me feel human again. It was also weird to know a lot about being messed up and have that be useful to others."

It was hard to turn the job down, but Chuck felt he needed to finish school. So after completing his own rehab, he returned to his dad's house. Returning home had its challenges. Part of rehab was agreeing to avoid communications with old friends, which Chuck abided. Being so far behind in school, because of his years of unruly behavior, made learning difficult and he was missing helping the guys in rehab. Since at that time, his sister was volunteering as a tutor for kids, he decided to see if he could get involved too.

One day when she went to the learning center, he tagged along. He took the test to see where his tutoring strengths would be, but the test showed 17-year-old Chuck had a third grade reading level. When the owner explained to Chuck that he could not tutor yet, but he could come to the center as a student and eventually gain the skills to be a tutor, Chuck jumped in.

"On my first day," Chuck said, "to my right was a 5-year-old girl and to my left was an 85-year-old man. We were all learning the same thing. I never felt dumb, because the room was filled with people of all ages. You never knew who was a tutor and who was a student just by appearance."

Chuck did eventually become a tutor for the center and graduated high school. He excelled once again and moved up through the ranks. He became an executive director for the center at age 19, and the unforeseen benefit of the center was the mentorship he received from the owner. She was a woman who had been a full-time volunteer in her thirties and decided to open the learning center to help people of all ages and all backgrounds. "There would be a homeless guy and a movie star's child in the same room getting tutored," said Chuck. While he was tutoring others, the owner of the center mentored him. "She taught me everything I know about running a business, working, public relations, and more."

Today, Chuck owns his own marketing and graphic design company. He started it six years ago, and it has grown every year in revenue. "We have experienced steady expansion of nearly double each year," he said. What's even more impressive is his clients are gained solely by word of mouth.

When I asked him what he was most proud of regarding his business, Chuck said, "I was able to take experiences of what I didn't like about the management styles at other jobs and create a fun, safe work environment for employees, that they love to work in." According to Chuck, it's not unusual for a Nerf gun to be used to settle disagreements.

Chuck had three mentorships impact his life: his step-mom who was the first person to really talk to him and try to understand, his own mentoring of newcomers to the rehab program, and the owner of the learning center who helped him succeed academically, professionally and personally. Because of those three experiences, Chuck is a successful businessman, happily married and has strong relationships with his family and friends.

Regarding mentorship, Chuck said, "Regardless of your life situation, having someone to look up to who will be there for you and answer any question is invaluable. Also, when you think you know it all is when you are the most lonely."

I'm sure you can think of situations in which you are familiar with mentoring being a useful resource. When struggling with addiction, addicts talk to sponsors. When struggling with grades, students work with tutors. When struggling with health or weight, people work with trainers and dieticians. Why is it that we search for help when we are challenged with something negative, but don't often search for help when working toward achieving something positive?

While on a Google Hangouts call with a mastermind group made up of entrepreneurs, I mentioned I had taken on a coach for authors. My new coach was mentoring me in getting a book ready for publication. One of the members of the group said she wasn't aware there was such a thing—an author's coach. My reply was, "I'm pretty sure there is a coach for everything these days."

For whatever goal you want to achieve, there is someone out there who has succeeded in it and can help you succeed too.

Look for someone who is successful at what you want to learn. It confuses me when I see people considering advice from an unexplainable source. Don't ask someone who struggles with money for financial advice. Instead, ask someone who is financially successful. An obese person shouldn't be the source of health advice just a someone with four divorces shouldn't be the source for marital advice. You have no reason to seek guidance from a source displaying contrasting evidence. Instead, build connections with those who are living what they recommend.

Whether it is home, work, relationship, financial, or health related, find a person who is doing well and ask if they'll mentor you. It can also be less formal; just ask if they are willing to connect a couple of times a month so you can pick their brain.

Create a mutually beneficial proposal. It's possible someone you ask will be willing to mentor you for nothing in return other than the intrinsic value they'll receive from helping another person. However, many mentoring relationships have a mutual benefit. Some examples include mentors being paid a fee for their time, getting an assistant when they take someone on as an apprentice who learns while helping them with work projects, or receiving value in a barter relationship. You mentor me, and I mow your lawn, babysit your kids, or build you a deck.

Listen and learn. To be a worthy and successful mentee, you'll need to develop listening skills. Hear what your mentor says with an open mind, be attentive, and ask follow-up questions. Otherwise, once a mentor realizes his or her time is being wasted with someone who isn't serious about growth, they'll likely sever the relationship, and you don't want to risk that after you've made the effort to get the mentorship.

Seek to understand *why* they do certain things, not only *how.* As you move through this ever-changing world, you'll need to know the whys, because the hows will probably shift and adjust over time.

Ask for sources of information. In some cases, you won't be able to get an immediate connection with people whose time you pursue. If that is the case the best thing you can do, while being patient for the chance or justification to fit into their schedule, is to ask for their recommendation of resources. If you want to learn from the best, and they can't work you in to their schedule right away, ask them to direct you to books, links, videos or other people they've found helpful. Once you've proven you are serious by completing their suggestions, they are more likely to give you their time or invite you to join their peer group.

You've come so far. Think of all you've already done: you've created a list of things you want to improve, you've performed acts of kindness for others, you've created an awareness around the strengths of those you spend time with in order to learn from them, and after the next action step, you'll have a list of possible mentors to reach out to. And you are only a third of the way through these chapters.

As you know, all of the improvements you make in your life, the vehicles that will take you to Destination Awesome, will positively affect you. It is so cool that those same improvements will also affect those around you.

It's time to take you down the second path that will lead you to your ultimate destination: The Path of Personal Characteristics. The next chapter will reveal how I became lacking in trust of others when I was five and continued to live skeptically through early adulthood. Though it was difficult to write and may be hard to read, I couldn't think of a better way to illustrate the topic.

Gone In 600 Seconds

Go back to the list you made at the end of Chapter 1, the changes you'd like to make in the next six months. Next to the desired changes, think of people already successful in those areas and write their names next to them. When you are ready, reach out to the people next to the first one or two you want to work on. Ask if you can set up weekly, bimonthly or monthly calls on which they can help you create a plan of action and discuss the results.

For suggestions on how to have the conversation asking someone for mentorship, see http://amieemueller.com/5-steps-for-interviewing-a-mentor-candidate/

The Path of
Personal Characteristics

Chapter 8

TRUST MAKES YOU STRONG

When considering your level of trust in others, how would you rate yourself? Very trusting? Very skeptical? And how does your level of trust affect your own success or happiness? Maybe you've never considered it has an effect. If you are like most people, your most common conversations about trust involve the level your parents have (or don't have) in you and the trust you have for and get from people you date.

Have you ever had someone mistrust you even when you've given that person no reason for it? How did it make you feel? How did it make that person look?

It may sound crazy, but just the act of trusting others can be beneficial to your happiness and reveal opportunities that would otherwise go unnoticed.

Beyond the neurological advantages to being trusting, which you'll read about later in this chapter, there are social benefits. I've found it impossible to experience a deep relationship with anyone if distrust is a factor. You will always be at least a bit closed off if you struggle to trust. Putting your trust in others, and being trustworthy, is a hinge in the door one opens to share his or her deepest insights and beliefs. Trust makes you a stronger companion and advisor.

Also, skepticism can hold you back from opportunities. Imagine if Mike Markkula (the angel investor and 2nd CEO of Apple Computers) had been too skeptical to invest in Steve Jobs' and Steve Wozniak's personal computer idea. His trust in those two men and their idea to create Apple computers certainly paid off.

As soon as you decide something or someone is not trustworthy, your mind stops searching for or noticing things to the contrary.

Bad Experiences and Their Effect

Generally, the level of trust we give to others is based on our past experiences. If you've had a lot of negative experiences with shady people, you are more likely to be skeptical. If you haven't had many of those experiences, you are more likely to be a trusting person, though neither of those generalities is true all of the time.

Experiences leading to my distrust of others began at age two with my parents' divorce and remarriages. Then took a dramatic downturn a few years later.

Often when my parents needed a babysitter, they'd leave me with the father of my step-mom. Any parent would have done the same; the service was free, by a trusted family member, and in a house on a lake, which was fun for the kids.

One evening, I was dropped off at his house. I was five and in his bathroom changing my clothes. I had stuffed one leg in my tights and was sitting on the toilet ready to stuff my other leg in when my step-mom came rushing in and grabbed me, yanking me forward. Dragging me by my bare arm, with my other hand grabbing the clothes pile on the floor, we barreled through his living room while she yelled, "I can't believe you did this," and, "How could you?" and, "You'll never see me again." It all passed quickly and without even knowing what was happening, I was in the car and on my way home. I wasn't sure what I had done to upset her and there was no time for explanation as we raced down the road.

I thought about never seeing him again. He was definitely not my favorite person, but he was generous and nice to me. He gave me more gifts than anyone else, he paid more attention to me than he paid to my brother, and he never yelled at me. Plus, I loved swimming in the lake.

I didn't know what it all meant. People were acting strange. My dad came home the next day, and he and my step-mom took me to the back room, away from everyone else, where he began asking me questions. Based on his questions, I knew.

They had found out the secret—the one my step-grandpa had asked me to keep. "Oh no," I thought. "I'm in trouble."

I didn't know what to say or how to act. I didn't know how to answer Dad's questions. I was embarrassed and uneasy, so I stood silent with a nervous smile on my face.

My dad stopped the flood of questions and yelled, "STOP SMILING! What is wrong with you?"

I was stunned. And hurt. And still silent.

What followed were more awkward conversations with my parents and a visit to a health center to be evaluated for proof of abuse. They gave me a sheet of blank, white paper and a crayon, and asked me questions to which they wanted my answers drawn out. I drew anatomically correct stick figures. They handed me a doll and told me to pretend the doll was me. The interrogation continued and I pointed to areas of the body on the me-doll to answer their awkward, personal questions.

Then the worst part of that day happened. I was put on a cold, hard examination table so they could do the physical exam. At the end of the evaluation, there was no doubt to the experts that sexual abuse occurred, but a legal battle never ensued, because my abuser died shortly thereafter from illness. After that day in the health center, my dad and I never spoke about it again. In fact, none of us ever spoke about it, and I never saw a therapist or counselor.

The mistake the abuser made, besides being a sick, law-breaking individual, was putting his hands on other girls. He'd also babysit the daughters of my parents' friends when the adults would go out together and we kids were all left at his house to play. Another girl, who had been left at his house on a previous occasion, shared what had happened to her and that she witnessed it happening to me as well. That was the night my step-mom came to my rescue.

As a child, I couldn't reconcile the injustice of the abuse with the confirmation of love or fondness by his other behaviors. What I do know is it set me on a path of distrust.

There were many times in my life in which people would remark on my response to their compliments of me. My reaction was quite puzzling. I either dismissed compliments as untrue or used them as evidence of the person's scheming. In my mind, if they were telling me nice things, they must want something from me. How would you feel if put in a position to defend an encouraging comment the way you'd be asked to defend a criticism? It made people uncomfortable and, therefore, unlikely to spend more time with me.

As a teenager, I also witnessed people in my trailer park, including my brother, using sex as a weapon or in selfish ways. I heard boys and men speak of their plans to trick women into bed. I saw women using promiscuity as currency to bend men to their will. I saw girls in school sob over broken hearts after giving their bodies to their boyfriends then being dumped. I also noticed the girls with the most suggestive wardrobes or sensual demeanors receiving the most attention from boys. To me, sex was something people did to each other with selfish intentions, and I had no desire to take part in it. I wanted a boyfriend and someone to love me, but I didn't want to be intimate. That carried over into my adult life and as you can imagine, it caused problems with my romantic involvements.

Reframing the Experience

Now that I've had time to reflect and work on letting go of the baggage, I believe there was a silver lining that came from my sexual abuse and perception of others' negative carnal behaviors. I was so disinterested in teenage sex that I wasn't one of the girls that battled pregnancy or STDs. My younger sister dropped out of high school when she became pregnant, some of the girls in my school did as well, and many teenagers today are dealing with those same consequences.

According to a 2012 article on American Teens' Sexual and Reproductive Health by Guttmacher Institute:

- 70% of teens (boys and girls) have had sexual intercourse by age 19.
- Each year, nearly 750,000 U.S. women ages 15-19 become pregnant.
- Although 15 to 24-year-olds represent only one-quarter of the sexually active population, they account for nearly half (9.1 million) of the 18.9 million new cases of STIs (sexually transmitted infections) each year.

I can appreciate that the negative correlations I had with sex helped carry me through and protect me during those confusing hormonal yet crucial years. Now, instead of heartbreak, I can experience gratitude for not becoming one of those statistics.

Distrust Can Cost You What's Most Important

Once I was older, and had talked with enough friends about it to understand sex was not always an evil thing, I participated in the act in my long-term relationships. However, true intimacy and vulnerability was still not a gift I gave to anyone. To me, letting someone close was foreign and scary, and it nearly cost me my marriage.

In our second year of marriage, my husband Josh read a book about creating a fulfilling life and one of the concepts was not settling for less than you really want. He asked me to join him on the love seat for an important conversation. Basically, he said, "We need to talk." I think we all know that is not a good sign.

He came to me with his assessment of our relationship. He was very calm. He didn't raise his voice at all. He explained what he read and how it gave him the courage to start the conversation we were about to have. He asked me not to interrupt, to listen until he was finished. I agreed.

He said, "I feel like you point out the things you don't like, but you don't ever tell me the things I do well. I don't feel supported. When I accomplish something I'm proud of, you don't congratulate me or celebrate with me. I need to hear you say that you love me and not tell me I should already know. I feel like I'm married and I'm still alone."

He continued, "I want more physical contact. And it's not just about sex. Yes, I want more of that too, but I want to hold hands and cuddle when we watch TV. I don't like it when you push me away when I touch you."

I sat there, silently, as I agreed to do. I was thinking about how I was going to respond. Nothing he said was untrue, so I just had to think of how to fix it.

He went on, "I don't want you to be someone you're not. I'm not asking you to change, but I also want to have these things. I've come to realize that I don't want to continue living the way I am now." Then he proposed to me for a second time. Only this time, it was a proposition to consider divorce.

I was stunned. I did not see that coming, and I didn't know what to say. He told me to think about it and we'd talk the next day or the day after. He went back into his office, and I sat on the love seat feeling very unloved.

The first thing I did was send an email to the author of that book. I had questions for him, to which I felt he owed me answers, since he was the reason my husband wanted a divorce. At least, that was my thought at that moment. I didn't really expect a response, but I got one and it was surprisingly kind.

I couldn't imagine getting a divorce. I had come to think of Josh and me as one unit. The idea of splitting up was so devastating, it plagued my thoughts the next few days. I could think of nothing else. Then a thought jumped into my mind, "maybe Josh and that author aren't the problem."

That is when I decided I needed to really deal with my issues. I didn't want to live a lonely life at my own causing. I asked my husband to give me some time to work on a few things. I assured him that I wanted all of the same things he wanted. I told him he didn't need to find someone else, because I could give him all of those things. I just had to figure some stuff out.

So I searched for answers.

Healing and Trusting

I chose to heal and let go of the baggage I picked up during my childhood. That was step one. After visiting with a counselor, reading books on the topic, and attending multiple personal growth and relationship seminars, I was morphing into someone new. It took months. Josh saw little improvements early on and was generous enough to give me a second chance. It was hard work, but the weight of mistrust had been lifted. I learned to let Josh in, to be totally open with him, and to be vulnerable. I learned to trust him, and to trust he would not hurt me even if I gave him the opportunity. Choosing to trust people left me free to relish in great friendships and a wonderful marriage, which leaves me feeling grateful, happy, and peaceful.

The Trust-Happiness Correlation

I know I'm not the only one who has had trust improvement needs. Have you seen people doing the trust fall exercise? It's where a few people stand behind someone. The person in front is usually on a raised surface and that person is supposed to willingly fall backwards with complete trust that the people standing behind will catch him or her. Why does it feel so alien to us to put our safety completely in the hands of others?

There are multiple videos on YouTube of trust experiments. Some involve handing out free money to strangers, and the surprising part is people won't take it! One such video is named

I've yet to meet a person who says they don't want to be happier. Even joyful people know there is always room for improvement or necessary effort toward sustaining their fulfillment. One path to that end is through trust. Many studies, including one by Paul Zak, director of the Center for Neuroeconomic Studies at Claremont Graduate University, show a connection between trust and happiness. One scientific relationship is that of oxytocin and trust. As we feel trusted, our levels of oxytocin increase, thus making us feel better and happier. It increases our happiness to feel trusted and to put our trust in others.

According to Terry Mizrahi, M.S.W., Ph.D., President, National Association of Social Workers, "Trust is at the core of all meaningful relationships. Without trust there can be no giving, no bonding, and no risk taking." If you want to be happier, you may need to increase your trust in others or in yourself.

Look for trustworthy qualities in everyone and you're more likely to find them. To view the world as conniving is to choose a life of separateness. Remember, most people want to be happy, loved, and fulfilled. Not every single person fits into the trustworthy category, but most do.

In general, begin any interactions with new people from a trusting perspective. Give them the opportunity to live up to your trust. If they give reason otherwise, being on guard in the future is an easy switch. Of course you should use your good judgment. I'm not suggesting you take part in questionable activities in order to demonstrate a trusting demeanor. Don't carry a backpack into an airport for someone you just met on the airport shuttle who says they'll meet you at the ticket counter!

However, you'll gain more by trusting early on than you'll lose by giving away trust too freely to those who don't live up to it.

Be trustworthy. Trust is a two-way street. Even if you are great at trusting others, if you are not trustworthy, your relationships will most likely fail. To be trustworthy, be a person of your word, keep your promises, be honest and be reliable.

Avoid stereotyping. If one man cheats that does not make all men unfaithful beings. If one priest molests a child that does not make all religious leaders suspect. If a woman cuts you off on the road, that does not make all women bad drivers.

To increase trust or happiness, you must not let an adverse experience frame your anticipation of future outcomes. Each person deserves to be judged only by their own actions, not by the entirety of your previous interactions. Consider someone's overall track record and have realistic expectations. Somerset

Maugham, one of the most successful writers of the 1930s, said, "Only a mediocre person is always at his best."

We all make mistakes. Step one is to realize no one is perfect. You can expect even the greatest person with whom you can imagine having a relationship will have reason to apologize from time to time. With an unrealistic perception people should never disappoint, they will certainly fail to live up to your expectations, and you will undoubtedly struggle to trust.

Be open with your communication. When communicating, share your feelings, listen to others' feelings with a non-judgmental ear, and be willing to consider new information. We all have things to learn and none of us is right all of the time. When a circumstance arises that tests your trust in another, commence with a conversation expressing your feelings. It's best to use diplomatic language. Your goal is not to attack and start a fight. The objective, instead, is to create an environment in which both parties feel they can open a dialogue without inviting defensiveness. You will probably find, in many cases, the other party didn't realize they were doing something that was not agreeable and are willing to change. Both parties need to be willing to grow and change when it's clear it will improve the relationship.

While having it for others is important, having trust in yourself and that you can achieve your goals is equally valuable. Before you can move forward in any journey, you must first decide what kind of traveler you will be. That is the subject of the next chapter.

Gone In 600 Seconds

Rate yourself in the following on a scale of one (lowest) to ten (highest)

- My level of trust in my friends _____
- My level of trust in my romantic relationships _____
- My level of trust in people I'm just meeting _____
- My openness when communicating with others _____
- My tendency to disbelieve stereotypes _____
- My own trustworthiness _____

For the areas that rate the lowest (or any below seven), take a moment to brainstorm why you rate it at that number and what you can do to improve in that area.

Check out other exercises and resources in the *Destination Awesome Action Guide* at the back of the book.

Chapter 9   # CHOOSING YOUR IDENTITY

hink of your response to this: tell me about yourself and how you
are different.

At the end of this chapter, you'll see why I want you to think about it.
In the meantime, let's talk about why knowing the answer is important to
your success.

Ruby's Story of Self-Reinvention

Ruby Ruth Willows was born on the Canadian side of the border between
Alberta and the United States. When fed up with her dad, her mom moved all
of his belongings into the yard, burned down his house, and left with her kids
headed to America. Ruby was only a toddler at the time. She grew up in a shack
with wooden slats for walls, struggled with poverty and scrounged for scraps of
bread from a nearby bakery.

As she grew older, Ruby noticed when others were around her or another
poor person they seemed to feel awkward; they found it hard to relate and felt
guilty for having more. Ruby decided she would reinvent herself. She did not
want to be viewed as poor.

On Ruby's 18th birthday, she went to enroll in the U.S. military and that's when she found out she wasn't a citizen. The navy enrolled her anyway, and she eventually earned her U.S. citizenship. She gave herself the gift of a whole new life, which she topped off with the bow of a new name. Ruby became Jan Willows.

The people who met Jan Willows would often refer to her as a woman who stood out. She looked at the positive side of everything, she was kind to everyone, and she had that special something you can't always put into words. Simon Cowell would say she had the X factor. She was the consummate host who went out of her way to make sure her guests were comfortable, to anticipate their needs and to relate to them. When anyone would comment on just how red her hair was, she'd respond, "I went through hell with my hat off." It was that kind of vibrancy for which she was known.

Ruby literally changed her identity along with her name when she became Jan.

Do Other People's Opinions of You Shape Your Identity?

How would you react if someone else described you and you felt he was way off the mark?

When I was in seventh grade, my school administrators put me in a special class. This decision was not based on my academic performance or my behavior. It was based solely on their perception of my home environment.

My older brother had one of the school's thickest student files. He skipped more days than he attended, he was a rebel to authority, and his drug use had become prominent. My father was only home two or three days out of every two weeks, so he wasn't able to enact discipline. My mother was absent from our lives more than my brother was absent from school, and my babysitters were usually teenage girls. The rest of my family's most prominent commonalities were teenage pregnancy, high school dropouts, drugs, and jail time. It's not hard to see why the school was concerned about my environment.

The special class was made up of at-risk kids from broken homes. There were ten of us chosen. We were the kids the school wanted to keep out of trouble, the kids the school wanted to keep calm, and most importantly, the kids the school wanted to keep away from the general student population. We even had our own secluded lunchtime.

It was not an environment of collaboration. We rarely spoke to one another and there was no group work assigned. Our teacher, Mr. Parker, taught us multiple subjects. The general class set up included a little teaching, an assignment, and time to work on it in class at our own pace. This class was designed to be an environment of very low pressure. It seemed Mr. Parker was charged with keeping the students as calm as possible. In that endeavor, he did a great job. There was very little stress in that classroom, and he was the perfect laid-back guy for it. I always wondered what he did to deserve the assignment of babysitting the class of us rejects.

Previously, I had performed well academically. Most of my report cards were cluttered with A's and a few B's. One of the things I'm grateful for is that I came into the world with an ability to learn quickly. So when we had the work-at-your-own-pace assignments, I was usually the first student to finish. I spent many days that year playing chess with Mr. Parker while the other students did their schoolwork.

When that school year wrapped up, Mr. Parker urged the administrators to put me back with the 'normal' student population. Admittedly, if he hadn't done that, I may have finished my junior high career in that special class. I was young, naïve and would never have considered questioning my authority figures. Mr. Parker swayed their opinions, and the following year I went back to regular classes, where I continued to excel academically. I went on to graduate high school in the top ten of the graduating class. To Mr. Parker, I will always be grateful for standing up for me and for teaching me to play chess.

As early as elementary school, I observed my classmates, and I knew there was something different about their lives. Since I only knew my home life, I didn't know what was conventional and to what degree mine was dysfunctional, but I knew they seemed happier. I knew most kids didn't have lice when I was fighting the infestations. At the after-school events, I could see most kids had two parents while I was alone. It was plain to see that other kids had nicer clothes, better school supplies, and were running in and out of doors to actual houses (not trailers), which I viewed from the window of the school bus. The point is

I knew I wanted what they had. So even though the administrators would not have purchased stock in me, I was going to fight to be on an upward trend. I may not have known how I was going to do it, but I would find a way.

The Identity that Saved Me

That day in fourth grade, when Mrs. Park told me I should go to college, had an impact on me. I had never considered college before she suggested it, but from that point forward, getting accepted to college was my plan. I believe it was partly the reason I focused on doing well in school. I decided very early on who I was: I was a girl going to college. It didn't matter what my environment was, how lacking my home life was, or if the school deemed me at-risk. I was on my way to a university. Every situation I ran into for the following nine years was viewed through the lens of being either helpful or hindering to that end, which is why that year with the *at-risk* class was totally off course.

As I shared in earlier chapters, drugs were a large part of my environment. My brother was addicted and when he was around, he and his friends were usually high. Pot was always in the mix, but he got into harder drugs like crack and meth. My step-dad was an alcoholic. Sobriety was rare where he was concerned. My step-mom was married to my dad for a few years and, after they divorced, she still made an effort to be in our lives. She remarried a man who was high almost every day, and she and her new husband would get high even during my rare visits to their home. It really upset me when my family would use drugs. I thought anyone who did was lacking in ambition or a healthy mind-set.

When I was a child, the sources of information I trusted were my teachers and pubic service television. Both of those were telling me that using drugs was wrong, unhealthy, illegal and irresponsible. So when I evaluated why we were seemingly stuck in circumstances not shared by others, and I witnessed an illegal, unhealthy, and irresponsible act being performed, it only confirmed what my teachers and anti-drug campaigns were preaching. I also have a hard time rationalizing how someone affords to buy any drug when they cannot afford other, more practical items.

As a teenager, I was the kid with no parents around, so a multitude of parties ended up at my place and were a chance for minors to experiment. There were parties at the trailer even when I wasn't there. It was more about the accessible location than the *host* of the festivity. For me, after seeing what drugs did to my brother, I was extra leery of them. The even larger issue was they didn't fit into my plans to get out of that trailer park. I was convinced by after-school specials that drugs were goal crushers, and my identity was a girl going to college. So all of the times I was offered cigarettes, pot or cocaine, my answer was always, "No thanks. I'm cool."

The Power of Identity

Adam Khoo, an entrepreneur, best-selling author, self-made millionaire by the age of 26, who owns and runs several businesses and is the Executive Chairman and Chief Master Trainer of Adam Khoo Learning Technologies Group Pte Ltd., said, "After working with more than half a million people in seven countries through my seminars and coaching sessions, I have found when a person makes a change and it lasts, it is because they did not just make a change at the behavioral, emotional or cognitive level, but they make a shift at the level of self-identity."

At a Tony Robbins event, I remember him saying being in alignment with one's self identity is a strong driving force in a person's decision making. Even a person's values and other beliefs will be secondary to it.

Let's say a person *identifies* himself as a social superstar and has a *belief* he should make healthy choices so he'll be around a long time for his loved ones. If he runs into a situation where he's offered an unhealthy option, such as a cigarette, in the midst of a group that is living large, and he feels declining will negatively affect his standing as the social kingpin, the identity will win out over the belief he should make healthy choices and he'll smoke the cigarette.

Celebrity Identities

A perfect example of this concept is Les Brown. When he was in fifth grade, he liked to clown around in class. When fed up, his principal referred to Brown as stupid and retarded. He was held back, required to repeat the grade, and Brown was labeled educable mentally retarded from that day forward. It was many years later when Brown's view of himself was challenged.

During Brown's junior year in high school, an encouraging teacher told him that someone's opinion of him doesn't have to become his reality. That statement changed his life. Brown said, "I finally realized the opinions of others did not matter. What was important was how I perceived myself."

Brown went on to do great things. He started out in radio and worked as a DJ. Later, he was elected to the Ohio State House of Representatives. Then he left the legislature to enter the world of television and motivational speaking. For a short time, he had his own talk show and won many awards, including an Emmy.

In an interview with *SUCCESS* magazine, Brown said, "In order to do something you've never done, you've got to become someone you've never been." Brown equates failing not to aiming high and missing but to aiming low and hitting it or not aiming at all. He went from being labeled retarded to teaching others a path to achievement. He changed how others perceived him by changing first how he saw himself. He got aligned with his identity.

I'm sure you've heard before that Michael Jordan's high school basketball coach said he wasn't good enough. Michael Jordan saw himself as a basketball player anyway. You've probably heard that one of Albert Einstein's teachers told him he was dumb. Albert Einstein saw himself as a scientist and a thinker.

Katy Perry, dubbed *Billboard's* 2012 Woman of the Year and the only artist to spend sixty-nine consecutive weeks in the top ten of the Hot 100, was not an overnight success. Her first two albums didn't do well. The main problem was her record company wasn't in agreement with her identity. The people in charge of her contract with Columbia records kept saying she needed to be the next Avril Lavigne or the next Kelly Clarkson. Katy said she didn't want to be the next anybody. She wanted to be the first Katy Perry—a girl with her own sound and style. Luckily, her manager was totally on board with Katy's ideas and helped her change record companies. Capitol Records signed her because they believed in Katy's vision, and when she was able to be herself, her success began to climb.

How You See You Matters

Your identity is who *you* believe you are. In other words, it's how you see yourself. How do you label yourself? Are you a great student or a bad student? Are you a hard worker or lazy? Are you smart or dumb? Are you a good or bad friend? Are you helpless or powerful? Dependent or independent? It is *you* who decides these things, not your circumstances.

The first step to achieving anything is to identify yourself as a person who can attain that objective. If you want to lose weight, see yourself as a healthy eater. If you can change your identity to that of a healthy eater, the choices you make from there will follow suit. Standing at the refrigerator with an apple and a piece of cheesecake staring back, a healthy eater chooses the apple. If you can stand there and think, "I am a healthy eater", and truly believe it, there is no choice. You grab the apple without putting your will power to the test. This is because your identity affects your standards, which affect your choices, which affect your actions. You act in accordance with how you see yourself.

In his book *The Charge*, Brendon Burchard writes of breaking out of the cage—the life you live knowing you could have more or be happier. He says, "It happens when we do the one thing that has ever helped anyone design a different destiny: consciously choose a new self-image, and fight to forge it into existence by consistently aligning our thoughts and behaviors to make it so."

In Larry Chiagouris' book *The Secret To Getting A Job After College*, he talks about the important first step: develop your personal brand. Larry has been called a branding guru and has appeared in hundreds of media outlets including *Fox News*, *The Wall Street Journal*, and *The Today Show*. He explains the importance of knowing your personal brand and how it's key to landing a position. Your brand includes how you dress, speak, carry yourself, and treat others, the characteristics you are known for, what you say when interviewers ask you to tell them about yourself, and how you differ from other applicants.

To me, your brand is having a clear understanding of your identity and making it known to others.

Katy Perry, Les Brown, and I found power in deciding who we were and not letting our environment or other people decide that for us. I know you will experience that same positive force when you make choices based on your chosen identity. Just as in previous chapters, in which you learned how reframing negative experiences can influence your happiness level, reframing how you see yourself can as well.

Vehicles to Take You to AWESOME

Decide who you are. Make a list of how you see yourself now. Be honest. Note the good and the bad. Self-awareness is helpful to creating the identity you desire. Once you have that list, you can decide what you want to keep, or even strengthen, and what you'd like to replace with something more cohesive to the best version of you. Write in those replacements and, after the exercise, your new identity will be defined.

Keep in mind your identity will adjust over time. When I was young, I was a girl going to college. After going to college, if my identity hadn't updated, I would have been lost. It's okay if you start by picking one or two things that you'd like to become part of your character. Even if you have ideas of many things you'd like to change, they don't all have to be done at once. Choose what resonates with you the most, what you feel drawn to, and start there. The last thing you want to do is overwhelm yourself to a degree where you can't take a first step.

If you aren't sure whether the characteristics you choose for yourself now will still be your desired identity years from now, that's normal. They don't have to be. What matters now is what you feel matters now. There is nothing wrong with adjusting it later, as you see fit. Learning to be self-aware and reinvent yourself, anytime you choose, are skills that will be useful for the rest of your life.

Visualize yourself in your new identity. If you want to be wealthy, picture yourself doing the things you'd want with your money. If you want to be a marathon runner, picture yourself wearing the number, see the crowds that line the streets to support you and visualize crossing the finish line. The brain reacts to both visualized stimuli and actual experiences. If you've ever awakened from a dream that had your heart pounding, or had your mouth salivate at just the thought of something sour, you've experienced the power of visualization. The more you picture yourself in your new identity, the greater the identity sets in our psyche, and the quicker you'll make the mental shift.

Act according to your new identity. Until it is part of you, you'll need to step out of your comfort zone. If you are currently fearful of public speaking but your new identity is that of a great orator, you'll need to push yourself to make those first speeches. You can start with small groups or by recording yourself, but you must take action. Adam Khoo said, "The moment it becomes comfortable, your new identity will stay."

Adjust your environment. Once you have your new identity decided, create a supportive surrounding. If you are a newly health-conscious eater, eliminate the temptation to eat bad foods by getting them out of the house and avoiding donut shops. Non-smokers have no need for cigarette cases or ashtrays. Going from a daily alcohol consumer to drinking monthly, weekly, or not at all? Ask your friends to meet you at a place where alcohol isn't served.

There will be an adjustment period. You won't decide who you are and wake up the perfect choice maker the next morning. Initially, create the supportive environment to make the choices easier. When your new identity solidifies within you, the environment won't matter. You'll be *who* you are no matter *where* you are.

At that point, you will be the thin, healthy person at the family reunion that only eats the nutritious potluck items despite having many less healthy options. You will be the person at the party who consumes zero to two alcoholic beverages and lacks the desire for more. You'll be the person at work that is calm even when those around you are agitated. You'll be the student who raises her GPA in both the tough and the blow-off classes. I know the power of knowing who I am. I am the girl labeled an unlikely success, academic or otherwise, by her junior high school who spent eight consecutive semesters on her college dean's list and graduated *summa cum laude*.

No matter how much you prepare yourself or how much you solidify your identity, doubts will creep in and attempt to dissuade you. Don't be fooled into thinking the most confident people aren't confronted with fears. They are. The next chapter will discuss how to deal with fear so it is only a pothole on your road to success, not a bridge-out.

Gone In 600 Seconds

Think about three things: how you want others to describe you, what would make you feel great about yourself, and what type of person would be likely to achieve the things you are passionate about. Related to those, what characteristics would that person possess? What behaviors would need to be displayed consistently? Don't limit yourself by thinking any of it doesn't describe who you are now. Write down that description. Include the characteristics and the behaviors.

If you choose, you can work toward making that depiction a real description of you. You don't have to become the entire identity at once. The first step is picking one characteristic or behavior and commit to making it part of who you are. So once you have that description written down, choose one thing you will implement immediately. Circle that one.

Continue with this and other exercises in the *Destination Awesome Action Guide* at the back of the book.

ACHIEVERS ACT ANYWAY

Chapter 10

E ach year, our junior high held a lip-sync contest. Students would choose their own teams and practice their routines for weeks. Then on the big day, they'd congregate in the gym, sit on wooden bleachers waiting their turns, and perform in front of the entire student body. Some students were audience members only, as it was not required to pretend sing, attempt to dance, or sport a funky costume.

I was close to invisible at that time, so who could blame the other kids for not asking me to join their teams? I was one whose shyness was teetering on social phobia. However, I did have one friend named Tracy, also not of the popular crowd, who wanted to put together a duo based on the 1988, first-ever single for Australian singer Kylie Minogue, remake of Little Eva's song "The Loco-Motion."

For weeks, Tracy and I practiced multiple hours each day creating and practicing a routine and counting down the days to our performance. In case you were wondering, neither Tracy nor I had any formal training in choreography, so it is safe to assume our act was going to knock the socks off of our peers and teachers.

As time progressed and opening night grew near, reality set in. I was not outgoing. I was deathly afraid of any criticism or unwanted negative attention this could bring if the audience didn't appreciate our unique composition of movement. I enjoyed the time spent with Tracy and the brief moments I believed I could actually do something so far out of my norm. I was having a lot of fun in rehearsals. However, when the day before the show became reality rather than just a square on the calendar, my anxiety took over, and I spent sixteen hours throwing up.

I had not ever before or since upchucked so fiercely over an extended period of time. I threw up so many times that eventually there was no food or liquid hitting the floor, only a greenish yellow slime. That's when I first heard the word bile. As you might have guessed, I did not always make it to the porcelain bowl. No one knew what was wrong with me. I heard suggestions thrown out including flu, ulcers, and gallstones, most of which would be weird for a 12-year-old.

Though I didn't want to admit it, because I was enjoying the attention, I knew what the problem was. I was allergic to performing in public. However, I kept that knowledge to myself and suffered quietly the understanding that fear was dispelling all nutrients and fluids from within. Amazingly, once the call was made to the school letting them know I would not be in that day—the big day—the vomiting finally stopped and I drifted off into a peaceful sleep.

I experienced the grip fear can have on a person. I hadn't learned how to battle it yet, and it left me with a raw, sore throat, but it was a lesson well worth living through. Experiences like that, early in life, are most likely the reason I've pushed myself to do many things that lead others to believe I'm a bit of an adrenaline junkie now. Since my early 20's, I've jumped from airplanes, fought through class five rapids, slid over mountain canyons on zip lines, faced Hawaiian waves on a surf board, walked over red hot coals, climbed fifty-foot twelve-inch diameter poles and taller cliffs, got up close and personal with sharks and sting rays, rappelled down rock walls, and have given public speeches to rooms with hundreds of audience members.

Defining Your Fears

What is your biggest fear? Is it heights? Spiders? Public speaking? An embarrassing viral video of you?

We all have fears, so if you were thinking you were the only one, you were wrong. When it comes to fears, there are two questions you have to ask yourself. Question one: Do any of my fears keep me from experiencing things I'd like to experience? In other words, do your fears hold you back? For example, if you are scared of spiders, unless you live in a place such as Australia's outback or in the forest next to Hogwarts, they are pretty easily avoided most of the time. So if you don't want to put the work into overcoming that fear, it probably won't affect any other area of your life. It shouldn't keep you from the career you dream about or finding the perfect life partner—unless of course his or her favorite thing is playing with spiders.

On the other hand, if your fear is flying and the career you'd like to have is related to international business or corporate consulting, that could be a problem. That type of career could require you to be a jetsetter at least part of the time. That means you would need to find a way to face that fear.

Question two: How do I feel about letting fear affect my choices? There is something to be said for overcoming fears no matter their role in your lifestyle. Even if you can avoid spiders, what is it worth to you to be able to act in spite of fears, any fears, you have? Some people aspire to conquer fear any time it arises regardless to what it relates. These people may even go as far as to seek out fear-inducing experiences just so they can feel the exhilaration of overcoming them. In doing so, they build up their fear fighting muscles as well as their self-esteem. I didn't start out as one of these people, but I found my way to this group, and I'm glad I did.

There probably isn't any rationale for walking on hot coals, but pushing myself to do it, in spite of how scared I was, was an experience I'll never forget.

Now that I think of it, there is a third question: If it's a fear I want to overcome, how do I do that? If you have any particular fears you'd like to overcome, or if you'd like to learn the strategy for overcoming any fear at any time, this chapter is a must read. It is filled with stories of how others have overcome their fears, and it will give you practical tips to doing the same.

Erik Sees Through Fear

Erik Weihenmayer is a climber. He climbed Mount Everest and has summited the highest peaks on each of the seven continents, which fewer than 100 people worldwide had done before. He is an accomplished mountain climber, paraglider and skier. Erik is a world-class athlete and the author of *Touch the Top of the World* and *The Adversity Advantage: Turning Everyday Struggles Into Everyday Greatness.*

There are many other adventurers out there. Some have completed the same or similar feats. The one thing Erik has that they don't, however, is blindness. He lost his sight at age 13 but didn't let it take his vision. Erik said, "You have to look forward and try to create a vision of what you're going to do. It will guide you when times are tough."

On the subject of fear, especially when doing something new, Erik said, "There is tremendous fear because, in a way, you are walking into a black hole and creating your own way forward. But that is where the excitement is." In cases of failure, he continues, "Sometimes if you fail and you learn some key fundamentals through that failure, it just gets you closer to what you want to do."

Since our future is unknown, to attempt anything is like looking into that black hole Erik described. We can't know what the outcome will be. We only know two things: what we want the outcome to be and that things will go unchanged if we don't at least try. The fear surrounding a highly challenging physical activity may have a different source than the fears most of us face every day, but they both have the capacity to stop us from getting what we want.

If we let them.

Loyd's Story—A Young Guy Faced with a Huge, Life-Altering Decision

Loyd was a mentor of mine for many years, and as impressed as I was with his many professional skills, it wasn't until he told me the story of his early adulthood that I learned the true strength of his resolve and character.

When Loyd was 17-years-old, he started working a sales position. He did very well and earned a lifestyle not many 17-year-olds have claimed for themselves. He even bought his first car—a Porsche.

He continued with that company for the next five years, moving up into management and eventually owning his own business. Shortly after starting that business, at age 23, his ex-girlfriend got in touch with him. She called because she was pregnant. If that wasn't scary enough for a young, new entrepreneur, what followed would certainly instill fear in anyone. She needed him to come to the hospital, because there were complications.

When Loyd arrived at the hospital, he learned there were some anomalies, which were going to keep the baby from forming in the usual manner. The umbilical cord hadn't attached correctly, so the baby's organs would form outside of the baby's body. The chance of infection was high and organ function was likely to be poor. The doctor told him the baby may not even make it through the pregnancy and if she did, she may not survive long after. If the baby made it into the world, she would need surgery immediately, and there would be no guarantee of success.

That situation would be hard enough on any parents, but at least most would have each other for support. That wasn't really the case for Loyd. He and his girlfriend were no longer a couple. After the doctor finished with his assessment and let them know they could consider abortion, they decided that wasn't an option they wanted to consider. Loyd's ex-girlfriend confessed that she couldn't handle being a mother at that point in her life, so there was really only one question left. Would Loyd take on the responsibility of being a single father or would they put the baby up for adoption?

Loyd said, "After the shock, the fears, and the pity party—the why me's— took their turns, I thought about how much I wanted to be a dad *some*day. Just because this wasn't how I envisioned it, didn't mean I shouldn't do it. So I decided, I was going to be a single dad."

Fortunately, the baby made it through the pregnancy, and even more luckily, the foremost expert on this particular anomaly happened to be in Loyd's city at a conference the day she was born. That expert agreed to go to the hospital and perform the surgery. Loyd saw his newborn daughter for about two seconds before she was rushed to surgery, but the surgeon turned to Loyd and asked, "What is your daughter's name? I want to be able to talk to her and root her on during the surgery."

After the operation, the doctor returned to tell Loyd he had just had the most successful surgery he'd ever had and that his daughter was a fighter. That was followed by six weeks of intensive care. It was on Loyd's 24th birthday he was able to take his daughter home from the hospital. Now he was a single father, with a baby heart monitor, a book of medical instructions, a new business, and a $200,000 medical bill.

New fears set in. How would he do this? Would he forget something important and hurt the baby? How do you get a baby seat in a Porsche?

Loyd took it day by day. He brought his daughter and all of the necessary medical equipment to work with him. He traded in his Porsche for a more baby-friendly vehicle. He worked hard at developing a staff that could handle things when he was busy with his daughter. He said, "It challenged me to get better at all areas of my business and personal skills, and as hard as some of those times were, my daughter and I developed a special bond through it all."

Loyd's business didn't skip a beat. He continued to grow in revenues, continued to earn new responsibilities and opportunities, he developed a great staff that went on to start their own businesses and be very successful, and he led his team to a national championship performance. He also found the woman of his dreams when his daughter was a toddler. This woman treated the child as if she was her own daughter and the couple went on to have four more kids. They are a happy family.

Loyd could have let the fear of being a single father stop him. The fear of handling a child with severe medical needs could have stopped him. The fear of being unprepared could have stopped him. The fear of building a business in the midst of it all could have stopped him. Any of those fears individually would keep some people from moving forward and he was dealing with them all at once. He is a true testament to the benefits of acting in spite of fear.

Erik and Loyd both had pretty large challenges to deal with, but sometimes the fear that accompanies even the smallest tasks can have a large impact on us.

Battling the Fear

Overcoming the fear of public speaking, for me, was a step-by-step process. After the lip sync debacle, I wanted to make sure my self-imposed weaknesses never stopped me again. My process began in high school when I took speech class. It was hard to stand in front of the room and deliver a message, but it somehow helped to know that everyone in the room would be put through the same torture. I figured they were all at least a little nervous too, so the likelihood of harsh critique was low while it carried the possibility of a subsequent backlash of criticism on their speeches.

Then I continued my growth by taking another public speaking class in college. Since I believed I was still more nervous than many of my college classmates, I decided the best way to get good results from the teacher and the crowd, while not being the most accomplished at actual delivery, was to share an interesting subject matter. I began putting a lot of effort into the research and crafting of my messages. While my classmates were delivering messages on the difference between manual and automatic cars and the ingredients in a pie, I delivered a message on cannibalism.

My topic might sound weird and maybe even grotesque to you, but it was a subject in the news at the time, so it caught my attention. And since I wanted to deliver a memorable message on a topic not covered in any other speech class, it fit the bill. And it worked! I got an A in the class and more than a year later, someone recognized me on campus. He said, "You're the girl who gave that cannibalism speech."

Me? Memorable?

That was a first.

The more positive feedback I received, the more I was encouraged to overcome my fear. It never went away, but I built tools to fight it. While still in college, I worked a sales job with Vector Marketing and did well enough that I started assisting in training other sales reps, so I got more opportunities to speak to small groups. I delivered at least a talk a month. Then as my confidence grew, I'd often get nominated to be the speaker in my class groups. No one else wanted to deliver the message and I was developing speaking as a skill. For each one, I was still nervous, still scared, but I didn't run out of the room vomiting, so they were all wins in my book.

In my experience, fighting fear is mainly a matter of preparation and focus. Once you've won the first battle, each one after gets easier and easier. You'll definitely be more scared the third time you speak in public than the thirtieth. At this point, I've given more than a thousand speeches.

To this day, I still feel fear's grip when I'm getting ready to take the stage, and the audience and the topic both have an impact on how intense it is. Recently, I gave a speech at a speakers' conference—a seminar for speakers to improve their speaking. So everyone there was a speaker, which meant they all had adequate knowledge and experience from which to judge other speakers. I was so nervous, I had muscle spasms as I waited for my name to be called. I thought they were all going to be able to see that I was nervously twitching.

The difference, now, is that I still walk out on that stage regardless of the battle fear puts up. Now, I act anyway. Though I didn't have the nerve to act in spite of my fear as a pre-teen, I have been determined, as an adult, to never let it stop me again. When you let your fear stop you from acting, you have found your limit.

The Relationship Between Fear and Courage

I never want to find my limit; I want to live a life that is limitless. Courage is an important quality of anyone pursuing daunting goals. While reading *SUCCESS* magazine, I was inspired by Laird Hamilton. Laird is a surfer from one of the most dangerous surfing regions in the world. He was one of the first to surf the eighty-foot waves in Hawaii and invented the tow-in surfing system, the process of being towed by jet skis in order to get to and from the waves unreachable with normal paddling.

In the magazine interview with Laird Hamilton, he negates the idea that he is fearless by saying, "I'm probably the most scared of anybody. That's the whole point." The article continues, "His daily hurdle is to overcome the fears and negativity that creep into his head each time he steps on a surfboard. Fear makes him a sharper thinker and forces him to make sound decisions."

Being courageous isn't the absence of fear, after all. Courage is taking action despite the fear. If there were no fear, there would be no need for bravery.

We all have fears. For you, it may not involve thunderous waves, fire walking, or junior high lip-sync contests. It might relate to taking steps toward the life you really want rather than settling on the one you're in. Are you scared of learning a new skill, talking to your parents about awkward and preferably unmentioned life topics, finishing school and stepping into the world of professions, being vulnerable with someone for which you care deeply, or one of many other matters? The point is, there is only one path to your goals and dreams, and it is through your fears.

Vehicles to Take You to
AWESOME

Focus on what you want and not on what scares you. If I had known to replace the thoughts of ridicule by my classmates with thoughts of how fun it would be to dance and laugh or how good I could feel about being there for a friend who was counting on me, I may have been able to calm my seventh-grade nausea. When I'm doing something that tests me, like jumping out of a plane at 12,000 feet, I focus on the details of my training, the equipment I am wearing, and the beauty of the landscape I am fortunate to witness as I plummet to the earth. The mind processes one thought at a time, so you just have to keep it focused on a positive outcome rather than the possibility of a negative one.

Act anyway. If you are unable to block the fears from your thoughts and are still experiencing a lot of distress, do what scares you anyway. You will never know the outcome if you don't. Most times, fear is a false outcome projection and is not the actual conclusion. For example, I'm sure nearly every new skydiver feels fear when the small aircraft door opens, they feel the rush of cold air on their faces, and hear the yells of their instructors indicating it is time to exit the plane.

However, in 2009, the U.S. Parachute Association recorded only 16 skydiving fatalities out of nearly 3,000,000 jumps made which included 400,000 first-time jumpers. That same year, the National Highway Traffic Safety Administration reported just under 31,000 deaths by motor vehicle accidents. Most people have a greater fear of jumping from an airplane than driving a car even if it's not statistically reasonable.

FEAR = False Expectations Appearing Real

If you can't stop the fear by focusing on a different outcome, act anyway. There is a good chance your fear will not be realized and you'll experience the exhilaration of achievement. Regardless of the outcome, you'll feel good for managing fear and displaying courage. The more you work the courage muscle, the stronger it becomes, thus making it less likely fear will discourage you in the future.

If you don't try at all, you don't gain anything. If you do try and fail, you're probably not worse off. In fact, at least you learned something new—what you tried that time doesn't work. In that case, on to the next try. If you try and succeed, you've improved your situation. Keep in mind, if you let fear stop you from taking action, you could end up with regrets. You'll never know how things would have turned out if you had taken action.

Fears generally come from within us, not from other people. Negativity can come from either source. If you've ever told someone about your goal and had them respond in a negative way—laughing at you, questioning your abilities, or labeling your goal as stupid—then you have experienced a type of negativity from others we'll discuss next. If you've had those thoughts yourself, you are experiencing negativity from within. The last step on The Path of Personal Characteristics talks about a way to deal with negativity and is covered in the next chapter.

Gone In 600 Seconds

List any fears keeping you from doing what you want. Decide which one you will battle first by acting anyway, and put a date next to it. That date will be your deadline to get it done.

For more exercises to help you face your fears, turn to the *Destination Awesome Action Guide* at the back of the book.

Chapter 11

DEAL WITH ADVERSITY

won't even ask if you've ever been given any criticism, because it has, without a doubt, been given to all of us. So instead, I'll be more specific and ask: what was the last piece of criticism you received?

And did it make you question yourself?

Feedback from others is a funny thing. On one hand, it can be a valuable tool, a way to analyze our impression on others. It can be a way of gauging our communication effectiveness and a way to involve others when a synergistic outcome is sought. Feedback is a necessary component in the communication equation.

However, you'll also get some feedback that is just plain useless, or worse, the kind that can be harmful. When it comes to feedback, whether it is useful or harmful is up to you to decipher.

Criticism Sensitivity and Its Effect

As a teenager, there were many things I would have loved to have changed about my appearance. Right at the top of that list was my fair skin. I have the type of outer coating that doesn't tan. If I'm in the sun too long without proper protection, I'll sizzle and end up as red as Dorothy's slippers. But once the outer skin peels away and the nerve endings stop shooting pain responses at the slightest touch, I'm left with skin as white as it was before the burn. My good friend Lisa would intentionally fry in the sun early each summer, because the red would turn to brown and she would have built a nice base tan for the next three months. I didn't have that capability.

As I mentioned, there were many things I didn't like about my physical appearance back then, but much of that has since been repudiated by people in my life. So though I always thought my nose was too big and crooked, my freckles were dorky, and my thighs were fat, I've learned those are not views shared by minds outside of my skull.

However, my skin color was one of the not-just-in-my-head attributes confirmed as a downside by others. For example, one day in high school, when I wore a pair of shorts to school, a group of girls in the hallway asked me why I was wearing white tights. With confusion displayed on my face, I replied, "I'm not." That led to giggling and pointing at my pale skin. That's when I realized they knew I was bare legged before they asked. That experience wasn't the only time such a comment was made in this regard, but after that day, the exposure of my bare legs was as uncommon as a Big Foot sighting and nearly as mythical. From then on, I usually wore pants.

To say I was sensitive to criticism during high school is an understatement. Any critique was taken to heart and devastated me. I feared negative feedback so much it kept me from doing things I desired. I didn't ask boys out on dates. I didn't speak up in groups. I wanted so badly to be a cheerleader, but never had the guts to even try out. As I grew intellectually, I came to realize the real problem with my skin wasn't its tint; it was its thinness.

When working toward goals you'll need to develop a thick skin, which means not being easily affected by negativity. To attempt anything important or take a chance going after something you really want, you invite the possibilities of failure, criticism and testing of your resolve. If your skin is as thin as my teenage epidermis was, it's going to increase the difficulty.

In Margarita Tartakovsky's article in *World of Psychology*, Ryan Howes, Ph.D, a clinical psychologist and professor said, "If you've had skin ripped away—[because of] trauma—or never developed thicker skin [because you were] sheltered from adversity, you'll experience every bump and sharp point with excruciating precision."

How do you like that? If you've had it too good or too bad, you are prone to higher sensitivity. I guess for those of us who are not in Goldilocks' perfect middle, we've got work to do.

Howes described thick skin as "the ability to adapt and roll with changes and challenges common to life, as well as the ability to bounce back from particularly difficult times."

Not everyone is going to be your cheerleader, and first attempts don't often lead to goal achievement, though they do usually offer new information and learning. My first attempt at love was also the first time I felt the sharp edges of prejudice. I was 14-years-old and when it came time to meet his parents, I was excited. I figured they'd be as smitten with me as he was. I was a good student, drug-free, tobacco free, and cared deeply for their son. Yet after that visit, and lots of coaxing for their opinion, my love shared with me that his parents didn't want him dating me. They weren't enthralled with the poor girl who lacked country club contacts. They met me for less than five minutes and had made that decision.

It hurt.

I didn't understand it at the time, but now when I look back, I can see how a pair of educated professionals living in a good home with a son on the golf team and a path to attend one of the state's best universities may not be enthusiastic about a girl from a broken home, living in a trailer park, whose family was known to have broken laws. Go figure. I may understand it now, but that doesn't mean their quick and biased opinion didn't feel like a knife to the heart then.

We continued to date anyway, and feeling like I won helped ease the pain a little. Can I get a cheer for teenage angst and misguided competitiveness?

Was there ever a time when someone was saying less-than-positive things about something you wanted to do? Have you ever had someone say you just couldn't do it? I think most people experience that at some point in their lives. My good friend Brett shared with me the story of a time when he dealt with painful criticism.

Brett's Story—When All You Want is What You're Told You Can't Have

Brett's father passed away when he was 4-years-old. For most of his life, it was just his mom and him, but she kept the memory of his dad alive by sharing stories. When Brett learned his dad had been an accomplished athlete, he wanted to follow in his footsteps and live up to his memory.

Just before Brett's freshman year of high school started, they moved to a new area, so he joined a new school. He was already a football player, but he decided he wanted to join the wrestling team as well. The challenge was that Brett was a 200-pound defensive lineman, and he'd need to lose 50 pounds to even have a shot at wrestling on the varsity team. When the coach shared that information, Brett decided he'd lose the weight, and the other boys on the wrestling team decided he was a lost cause.

Many of the wrestlers told him he was never going to do it. He couldn't do it. The other boys who would be his teammates, if he made the team, said, "You're a fatty," and "You'd be wasting your time to even try." At times, he was ridiculed in the lunchroom and scrutinized no matter which foods he put on his lunch tray.

Luckily, Brett wasn't the only new kid in school that year. Another boy named Brandon had just joined the same class and he was an excellent athlete. "He was the kind of guy who made it look natural," Brett said. The two newcomers became friends and started training together.

Brett revamped his diet completely. He started eating healthier than he ever had before. He and Brandon would train, and Brandon would help keep Brett motivated by putting awards in place for achievement milestones and using of words of encouragement. Brett also cut stories out of the local newspapers that recognized top athletes. He kept a scrapbook of those and reviewed them to remind himself of his goals.

By the time weigh-in day arrived on the calendar, Brett knew he had made progress. His reflection in the mirror, looser fitting clothes, and an overall increase in strength was proof of his improvement. The question was… had he lost enough? Would he be able to try out for the varsity team?

Brett walked to the scales, his nerves camouflaged by the confidence he projected. He watched intently as the technician read the results.

The verdict: he hadn't lost fifty pounds.

He lost fifty-three.

Brett not only tried out for the varsity team. He made the team. He went on to have a great season, which ended with him sitting as an alternate at the state competition. From there, Brett went on to compete at the state level for the next three years of high school and became a collegiate athlete on the wrestling team at Oklahoma University.

"That wasn't the only time I experienced such a thing," Brett said. "When I tried out for men's choir my freshman year, I was told I needed another year of lessons, that I wasn't good enough yet. Then the leader of that choir was fired and the person who took that position gave me a spot. I ended up being an all-state choir singer and was the youngest member ever to spend a summer touring other countries with Vocal Majority, a traveling men's choir."

When I asked Brett why he thinks people were critical of him and why they doubted his likelihood of success, he said, "Criticism can be vocalized potential. If there is an area that you need to improve, criticism can be a good thing, a direction for your effort. It can be helpful. Sometimes, though, critics are just selfish. It makes them feel empowered or in control by hurting others."

And how did he stay focused on what he wanted rather than being defeated by ridicule or negative feedback? "I always cut out pictures of what I wanted to accomplish and put them somewhere I could see them. It kept me focused. Also, you can usually find supporters of your goals. Not everyone is a critic. Find the people that support you and let them. Lastly, you should accept criticism, but you have to evaluate for yourself whether it is accurate and helpful or whether it is just negativity. Either way, don't let it stop you."

Criticism Only Has the Power You Give It

Eleanor Roosevelt said, "No one can make you feel inferior without your consent." If you chose to reach out to others for their feedback, as suggested earlier in this book, you certainly know how it feels to be evaluated by others. You probably already knew how it felt, since it's unlikely that was the first time you ever received others' opinions of you. Though, it may have been the first time you requested it.

Even when you ask for feedback, it can still be painful to get. If you ask someone to punch you in the stomach, it's still going to hurt whether you requested it or not. However, keep a few things in mind. It's up to you to evaluate the accuracy of their feedback. They've only seen what you've let them see of you while you were in their presence. So if you've never shown them your finest attributes, they won't know you possess those qualities. If they saw you in one of your darkest hours, they may not know they witnessed you during a time when you were not your normal self.

I'm not suggesting you disregard all feedback as inaccurate based solely on the limited amount of time that person has spent with you. I am suggesting you evaluate any opinions with some logical thought and deduction. If they believe you are a certain way, and you disagree, then figure out which of your behaviors they witnessed that gave them that sense of you. Then you'll know which actions to adjust or avoid so you don't continue to give a misguided impression.

Feedback is useful when you want to learn from it. It is not useful if you let it define who you are or make you feel bad. "They say I'm stupid, so it must be true," would be the wrong way of utilizing criticism. "They say I'm stupid, so I must figure out a way to show people I am smart," would be a much better use of feedback, if intelligence is something you want to exhibit. Your reaction to criticism will always be in your control.

People can't see inside your mind or heart. You may experience unjust criticism, of which you'll need to resist the effects. You also may experience accurate criticism, which you'll need to learn from rather than let devastate or end your quest. Sometimes, it may be more difficult to achieve your goal than initially thought, and you need to remember, without a doubt, it's not a sign you should quit but rather a sign you need a new strategy or stronger resolve.

On the UK television show *X-Factor*, some young gentlemen tried out for the competition. The judges told each of them they were not good enough to make it as individual singers. However, the judges did believe they were talented enough to make it as a group and should consider joining together. They did become a group and finished the competition in the show's finale and in third place. Prior to the show, the boys had never met.

After the show, they were the first British band ever to debut their album at number one. In addition, their second album released in 2012 had already gone platinum by the end of that year. That fall, they performed at two sold-out shows at Madison Square Garden. That group is One Direction, and their first big hit was "What Makes You Beautiful."

If the young men had let the judges' opinions that they would not succeed individually devastate them and reject the idea of becoming a group, they would not have the mega success they've experienced. Instead, they took the criticism, learned from it, found a new strategy, and continued on the path to their dreams. Of course, they are not the only success story that came after failure or heartbreaking criticism. There are countless examples. In Chapter 1, you read a list of people who didn't let negative circumstances keep them from their dreams. Here are a few of the most famous examples of people who didn't let negative criticism stop them.

- Albert Einstein's teachers told him he was mentally handicapped. He would go on to win a Nobel Prize.
- Vincent Van Gogh sold only one painting while he was alive, but didn't let that stop him from continuing his craft.
- Stephen King's first book was rejected thirty times before someone agreed to publish it. Now he has more than 50 published novels and has sold more than 350,000,000 books.
- Thomas Edison once said, "If I find 10,000 ways something won't work, I haven't failed. I am not discouraged, because every wrong attempt discarded is another step forward." It's good for us that he felt that way considering his estate holds more than 1,000 patents on inventions. Imagine if he had given up after the first few hundred attempts on the light bulb. It would be a much darker world.
- J.K. Rowling, the author of *Harry Potter,* said, "You might never fail on the scale I did, but it is impossible to live without failing at something, unless you live so cautiously that you might as well not have lived at all—in which case, you fail by default."

Know that you will fail. Your two choices are: 1—to fail, learn, try again, maybe fail again and learn some more, try again, and achieve and 2—fail to even try. Letting failures deter you from your dreams *must* be avoided, not failure itself. On your path to achievement, thick skin is your armor while connections, choices, and continued growth are your tools.

In his book, *The 15 Invaluable Laws of Growth*, John Maxwell says, "Growth always comes from taking action, and taking action almost always brings criticism. Move forward anyway. To reach your potential, you must do not only what others believe you cannot do, but what even you believe you cannot do."

In that first sales job selling Cutco Cutlery, during college, I was taught that every "no sale" got me closer to the next sale because of the law of averages. Therefore, a rejection from a customer was transformed into positive anticipation. Regardless of the sales outcome, I didn't take it personally. As long as I did my presentation well and gave no reason for them to dislike me, a customer choosing not to place an order was not a criticism of me but a matter of imperfect timing or a lack of interest in a particular product.

I learned a lot about not taking rejection personally and trying to see other points of view. I did so well selling Cutco, I paid my college tuition and my personal bills during school, which allowed me to graduate debt free. I did not take out student loans even though I was on my own to fund my education. I also took a promotion with the company and helped train other sales representatives, while maintaining and growing my own customer base. That leadership position revealed, to me, more areas for improvement. As the opportunities for my leadership and use of communication skills increased, I realized the undeniable necessity to begin a serious process of self-development.

Now I welcome criticism; I even ask for it. Many times, I've reached out to people I worked for or with, asking for their evaluation of me in different areas. I've taken various personal assessments to determine areas for improvement. Each time, I seek the good and the bad so I know what to continue and what to develop. I went from doing everything I could to avoid criticism to inviting it. My skin will never get darker, so though it's not much protection from the sun, its growing thickness does provide a barrier to life's jagged edges.

People will disappoint or hurt you and it will test your ability to remain trusting, your environment will test your commitment to your empowering identity, your own fears will test your strength of focus and action, and critics will test your resolve. You can pass these tests with flying colors, and you don't have to do it alone. You've got all of the people in these pages setting the examples and reminding you of your courage and your capacity, and you can come back and review these topics or stories any time you need a boost.

Vehicles to Take You to
AWESOME

Realize failures and feedback are necessary parts of the success formula. Develop a thick skin so adversities and critiques don't dissuade you from attempting to achieve your dreams.

To develop a thicker skin: focus, make a list, take action, and post your goals. *Focus* on the lessons learned from any setback rather than the obstacle itself. *Make a list* of past accomplishments and keep them in an accessible place. When you come up against a challenge, take a moment to review the list. Hold on to some tokens such as trophies, awards, photos of great memories, letters of thanks or commendations and remind yourself what you are capable of despite adversity.

Concentrate on your *actions* rather than your shortcomings. Even the most successful people have weaknesses, but they focus on what they need to *do* next rather than those deficiencies. Taking action leads to progress as long as that action is related to overcoming personal limitations or taking steps toward your goal.

Goals should be continually in your mind and view. *Post them* where you'll see them often. They can be written out or in picture form, and taped up around your house, in your car, on your phone, on your desk, or anywhere else you'll see them daily. Constantly remind yourself what you're striving for and obstacles will become temporary delays on the road to victory.

Evaluate criticism with a logical mind, not an emotional one. Ask yourself why that person would criticize you and what makes them qualified to have an opinion. Are they trying to be helpful or hurtful? Are they qualified to give you feedback in that area? If they are qualified and trying to help, consider heeding their feedback. If their credibility or intentions are questionable, consider politely ignoring it. In either case, try to avoid a negative emotional response.

We've finished the second route. It's time to map out the last one—The Boulevard of Behavior. You are doing a great job. Your commitment to the action steps in this book is commendable and exciting since you're already making progress by doing them. You know how to get closer to your objectives by implementing trust, choosing your identity and overcoming fears and negativity. Now we'll move into how your behavior impacts your success.

Gone In 600 Seconds

Make two lists: first, write down five to ten accomplishments of which you are proud. Next, write down one to three goals you'd like to accomplish in the next six months and why. The why is what accomplishing it would do for you—the reason behind the goal.

Put these lists somewhere you'll see them every day. Then take a picture of them with your phone, so you can take them with you everywhere. When you face negativity or doubts, review these lists. Your accomplishment will remind you of your capabilities and your goals and whys will help motivate you.

For more exercises, turn to the *Destination Awesome Action Guide* at the back of the book.

The Boulevard of Behavior

Chapter 12　　　GET MORE FROM DOWN TIME

D o you ever feel overwhelmed? Maybe you feel like you have a lot to do and not enough time to do it all. If so, you are not alone. In a study by the American Institute of Stress, they found that 66% of people said the two main causes of their stress were their workload and juggling it with their personal lives. If professionals are finding it hard to get it all done, and they are generally older and experientially wiser than young adults, what does that say about people with less experience being able to handle their workloads?

I'm passionate about this topic because of both my personal experience and my belief in your capabilities. As a young adult, I was completely on my own—financially, socially, and academically. I had a job at fourteen and from fifteen on, paid bills and managed a bank account, prepared my own meals, drove myself to school, managed my academic responsibilities and made all of my own social decisions without the input of any parental units. I did all of that while earning A's in school, showing up on time to work, and never having an unpaid or late bill. So I know what young people are capable of.

Developing certain habits while you are young will affect you for years. That applies to both good and bad habits, by the way. I don't think the years in your experience define you as much as the experience in your years does. Therefore, just because people who are older than you may struggle with their work/life loads, it doesn't mean you can't find ways to get it all done.

The challenge for many young adults transitioning to living on their own is they are usually new to handling *all* areas of their lives. They have to handle things previously taken care of by a family member. These could include transportation, living situations such as paying rent and other bills as well as relationships with roommates, household activities such as laundry, grocery and other shopping, cleaning and cooking. Furthermore, they'll be making all of their social choices, no longer having to get permission from anyone. They make *all* of their own decisions. Worry of not being able to get it all done, and done well, is commonplace.

In mentoring hundreds of college students, I found an area that really helped them get more done. It was making use of unproductive time, especially the time of which their participation isn't by choice but is a requirement. One example would be the time between classes. No matter how hard they try, students can't always get classes to fall back to back in their schedules. It's likely they'll have a break between classes—a break long enough to make useful but not long enough to leave campus and return before the next class. Some students will not use that time productively and instead will kill time surfing YouTube or Facebook, playing games or something similar.

Managing your time better so you don't constantly struggle with feeling overwhelmed or consistently miss deadlines is a matter of a few simple techniques. If you don't want to be part of that 66% who feel stressed out by their workloads, you don't have to be. Negative stress is not a requirement for success or achievement.

Chad, one of the college students I mentored, came to me after we had worked together for about seven months. He asked if we could meet in my office and talk. I agreed and prepared myself to receive bad news. I think most of us do that when someone says they need to talk in private, right? We sat down at my desk, and Chad told me he had just gotten his semester grades. "I got all A's. I've never done that before." He went on to tell me that he was certain the time management he learned from me was the main reason for his academic success that semester. "Thank you, Amiee!"

I didn't know what to say. I was relieved he didn't have bad news. I was happy he was happy and succeeding, and I was touched he was thanking me for something I believe was all his own doing. I may have taught him the techniques, but it was totally Chad's choice to put them to work, to make the commitment, and to be disciplined so he could move toward his desired destination. Being able to witness people growing and see their delight when they succeed is my favorite part of being a mentor.

Marc's Story—A Major Shift in How Time is Spent

Marc always wanted to stand out, and as a teenager, it wasn't as important to him whether he stood out as the best or the worst as long as he was noticed. And who could blame him for lacking great decision making skills early on? His dad left when he was a toddler, and for most of his childhood, his mother dealt with alcohol and drug addiction. Marc had to watch as she was arrested and part of several interventions.

When his mom remarried, the man was a great father to Marc, and he and his step-dad became close. One of the hardest things Marc ever had to do was keep his mother's adultery a secret from his step-dad. Can you imagine having to lie to someone you love so you don't lose him while keeping the confidence of someone else you love? That tore Marc up inside, and he started acting out.

In high school, Marc started disrupting his classes and cheating. He was eventually kicked out of school. When he transferred to a new school, he fell in with a bad crowd and things got worse. Marc began selling drugs, making fake IDs, committing credit card fraud, being involved in burglaries, and eventually robbing banks. He was arrested multiple times before he graduated high school.

When graduation arrived, it wasn't a time of celebration, because it was at that time Marc's mom overdosed. Following the funeral and graduation, Marc left for New York to go to college, where he continued his criminal activities. Shortly thereafter, his trial for previous offenses took place. He was convicted and ordered to move home to Texas where he would serve his probation and community service hours.

While Marc was in high school, he had taken a job in order to have a legitimate source of income. The legitimacy was only to hide the money he was making illegally. So when the judge ordered him back to Texas, he returned to the same company for work. He was on a work-release program on the weekends and attended college classes during the week. Though he was doing well at work and on a short list of people up for a promotion, he continued to party most nights and was doing hard drugs. During that first year on probation, he was caught with drugs in his car. Probation was revoked and Marc was sent to jail. By that point, he had thirteen felonies on his record. In addition, one of the guys Marc partied with ended up fleeing the country on the run from the law. He was eventually caught in Belize, which was all over the news.

Marc's family had given up on him, saying he'd never change, but his managers, at his legitimate job, hadn't. They vouched for him in court, and one of them kept in touch while Marc served his time in jail. That man became Marc's mentor and helped him gain a whole new perspective. Marc decided he wanted the life of success, fulfillment, and helping others that his mentor had. He wanted to prove wrong everyone who said he'd never change, and he didn't want to end up the way his buddy did—a fugitive on the news.

Marc decided while in jail, he would still work for that promotion that he missed out on when sent to jail and get back on track to his Destination Awesome. He determined he'd use the time to perfect his craft and leave jail on a mission for greatness. He wanted to make his family and those managers who vouched for him proud. So he spent his incarcerated time reading, studying, preparing and keeping in touch with his mentor.

It worked.

When he was released, he was assigned to probation for another five years as well as five hundred hours of community service. He stayed sober, passed all of his drug tests, and no longer participated in criminal activities. He did get that promotion, and it led to even bigger promotions down the line, which is where I met him. Today, Marc is a Division Manager in a multi-million dollar marketing company. He leads a team of more than fifty people at multiple levels of the business and trains other managers who lead their own teams. He has reinvented himself so completely that no one would guess his background is fraught with corruption.

When I asked Marc how he went to jail as one guy and came out of jail a new person who continued to improve, he said, "Some of it was a natural progression to maturity, I suppose. I realized we can do whatever we put our minds to. We just have to decide to use that toward something good, not criminal." He continued, "I committed to personal growth. I read a lot. I always have a book at work and at home. I listen to audio books while driving, and I got myself a professional coach. All of those things helped me stay on the right path."

Marc is a great example of making the most of what others let pass as unproductive time. Many people, who are incarcerated, do not find productive ways to use their time. Marc used it to work toward a new, positive life. You may not be incarcerated, but are there times when you could be more productive if you chose to? Even if it's time your peers don't make useful, you still can.

My Experience With Wasted Time

To get a clear picture of where I spent some of the most disappointing times of my life, you have to first picture a set of plastic stairs—three steps, about three feet in length, all protruding from the same rectangular, plastic base and sitting in front of a mobile home. When I was four-years-old, I sat there next to a small bag of clothes.

After my parents' divorce and conversation about custody, guardianship of my older brother and me went to my dad, who agreed to not collect child support from my mom if she didn't put up a custody fight. My dad also made sure we were available for visitations with my mom because he thought it was important we maintain that relationship. My mom was eight years younger than he was and wasn't as stable a guardian since she didn't have her own home or job at the time. These, of course, are all details I learned later, as I was a toddler when "till death us do part" no longer applied to them.

There I sat, on the once white stairs, waiting for her to pick us up for her weekend with us. I sat for hours. Any car that drove near sent a wave of excitement through me, but as it drove past and I realized it wasn't her, the anticipation turned to sadness. The daylight and my hopes would fade simultaneously, and I'd greet the night with a broken heart and a flood of tears.

The experience was worse for my brother who was a little older and had a better understanding of what was going on. This happened many times, and each time I'd go into it with an expectation that she'd show up and be disappointed when she didn't. Why I didn't learn my lesson quicker is still a mystery. You'd think I'd have learned not to sit and wait for her.

I went through difficult emotions in that process, but happiness wasn't the only thing my mom stole on those days. The amount of time wasted was as big a loss. Time is a limited resource. We can't buy more of it, slow it, re-use it, or recycle it. When it's gone, it's gone. Obviously children aren't expected to put strategies for productivity to work, but if 4-year-olds had any concept of time or opportunity costs, I would have put those hours to better use. Rather than sitting for hours, I could have been climbing trees, annoying my brother, or running around with other kids in the trailer park. At any age, the concept still holds true. Had I been doing any of those other things, my focus would have been elsewhere, thus lifting some of the weight of waiting for her, and I wouldn't have to look back at that time as such a waste.

Making Better Use of Down Time

Not long ago, I passed a group of campaign signs displaying various politicians, pulled into the elementary school lot, parked my car, and joined around fifty people in line to cast a vote in the presidential election. As I walked toward the crowd, a lady said to me, "Good idea bringing a book." For the forty-five minutes I stood in line, I polished off quite a bit of *The Go Giver* by Bob Burg and John David Mann. Each time I looked up to check out my surroundings, I noticed every other person in line either staring into space or fiddling with their phones as we shivered in the cold breeze.

Maybe you've experienced something similar. When waiting on your girlfriend to get ready, waiting on or for the bus or train, waiting in line at the DMV or Starbucks, what do you usually do with that time? I'm not saying you have to be productive at all times, but people often say to me, "I don't understand how you get so much done," and this is one of the reasons.

I'm much smarter with the time I spend waiting than I was as a child. You probably are too.

When I'm at the doctor's office, I'm working on a speech or reading a book in the waiting room. When I'm waiting on oil to be changed in my car, I'm preparing work for our employees or checking emails. When I'm waiting for dinner to finish cooking, I wash dishes and often listen to personal improvement messages online. Recently, I was alone on a 20-hour road trip, and I listened to an entire novel and forty TED talks. I would have been disappointed if the only thing I could have done with the twenty hours was drive. Instead I was able to learn and be entertained.

Another great example is Josh's mobile office. My husband does sales, consulting and coaching, and he travels to see his clients. On occasion, one of his appointments will be rescheduled or cancelled at the last minute based on the customer's timetable. Josh carries his laptop, prospect files, and power adapter in his vehicle. No matter where he is, if his schedule changes, he can use that time to call new prospects or work on his computer. He does not put himself in a position to be losing time when he would prefer to be productive.

There is nothing wrong with using your waiting time as down time, if you need to decompress. Everything has its place in your schedule. However, if you already have leisure time planned elsewhere, why not send a few appreciation texts out to people you care about, read ten pages of a book that teaches you something new, listen to an audio file, make a call that could add a check to your to-do list or one of many other things that could increase your productivity or enjoyment?

John Maxwell said, "Time has a way of getting away from most people, yet time is what life is made of. Everything we do requires time, yet many people take it for granted. How you spend your time is more important than how you spend your money."

So again, I honor you for taking the time to read this book, and I appreciate how important your time is. Continuing to use your time wisely, by doing things that will help you get to your desired destination, will help you achieve great results the same way it helped Chad get his best grades yet, Marc get his life back on track, and Josh continue to roll with the punches in his business.

Vehicles to Take You to
AWESOME

Have a to-do list. You've probably heard this before. I've read it several times, yet it is a great tip that many underestimate. The only reason I can remember to do all of the things that need doing is because I keep a list. I check it every day, multiple times a day. It gives my mind a break from having to remember every detail. Once things are done, they get scratched off and as new things come up, they get added.

Keep it on your calendar, in your phone, on a post-it note, or anywhere else you can look often. For most people, on their phone is best for easy access. The format isn't important, so whether you use the notes on your phone or download an app is personal preference. I have the Wunderlist app now. I used the margins of a paper calendar for years. What matters isn't how you keep it, it's that you make it and have it accessible.

Make use of down time. When you find yourself between activities, look over your to-do list and see what can be accomplished. We all have times we are forced to wait on someone or something, but we are never forced to do nothing while we wait. We have a choice. If you take action only when prompted by someone or something else, your productivity will always be determined by your circumstances, and that is not the way of achievers.

Carry useful tools with you so you can make use of down time. It's easier than ever, since books and podcasts can be downloaded to your phone. It's great to get more done in the same or less amount of time. When I do, it makes me feel empowered, and that is always a good result.

Implementing the aforementioned ideas will help you be more productive. The next chapter addresses whether it is better to blend in or be different. As you read it, reflect on your own actions with regards to fitting in or standing out and decide which is more likely to help you get to your desired destination.

Gone In 600 Seconds

If you don't have a to-do list, make one. Even if you don't have a lot to put on it at this very moment, at least get it set up for future entries. Download an app or title a phone note as To-do List.

Then enter anything and everything on that list that you want to get done. Examples could be: research for school paper, laundry, get oil change, find a professional in an area of study I'm interested in and set up a time to interview her about her job and industry, schedule a meeting time with my study group, call mom or dad for a quick chat, review bank balance on line, study for upcoming test, or plan a night out with my friends.

Review your list daily at a minimum. Any time something else comes up or you agree to do something for someone, add it to the list immediately so you won't forget.

Chapter 13　　BE BETTER THAN AVERAGE

t was fifth grade when the concept of popularity and conforming worked its way into my awareness. For the next eight years, my greatest desire was to fit in. I didn't like living in a trailer while the other kids lived in houses. I was embarrassed to wear second-hand clothes while other girls were wearing pretty outfits.

Since I was broke, I didn't get invited to birthday parties, and while everyone else was on a field trip to Washington D.C., I was one of five kids too poor to come up with the money, and therefore, went to empty classrooms instead of our capital. Seeing how my stuff compared to others, I avoided sharing when the teachers would ask about summer vacations or family show and tell. I never felt like I fitted in.

One day in fifth grade, our teacher was reading brainteasers aloud for the class to solve. She would express a scenario and ask us why or how it occurred. The students would ask questions or guess, and she would respond and give clues until the correct answer was given. I still remember a few of them. It made a big impression on me, because they were interesting, fun, and like nothing I'd heard before. The first one she shared was, "Two men had drinks together. One man drank his right down while the other sipped his beverage. A short while later, the man who drank slowly was found dead. What happened?"

After the class asked many questions and gave a few incorrect guesses, it was determined the ice was poisoned. Drinking it slowly gave the ice time to melt and release the poison into his refreshment.

As the teacher went on to give us more problems to solve, I caught on to the process and began solving them more quickly. She announced a man had a dream his work building was burning down then woke up and realized it was actually on fire. So he called for help, and after a team put out the blaze, he lost his job. She asked us, "Why was he fired?" I whispered to the classmate sitting next to me, "He was sleeping at work." My classmate raised her hand and repeated it to find out she was right. For the next question, I whispered an answer again. Only this time the teacher noticed and called me out for talking in class. Drat. My longing to fit in was greater than my longing to be right or clever. If most of the kids in class didn't know the solution to the puzzle, I certainly wasn't going to be the one to exclaim it. To be normal, that was the goal.

The Norm or Not the Norm? That is the Question

It's sort of funny how much of our adolescent lives are spent trying to fit in. Even for the people who want to be different than the majority, they still want to fit in with their own crowd. Then after years of training in blending in, you are told as a young adult that if you want to get accepted to your choice of school or hired for a job, you'll have to stand out. It's like you arrive at this day in your life on which you are expected to do a complete one-eighty without missing a step. And no, Ashton Kutcher and the cameramen of *Punk'd* are not going to be there when it happens.

That one-eighty means your training up to then is inadequate and you have a new set of skills to develop. As weird as that expectation may seem, it's true. If you want the gems of life, exhibit the unique qualities that make you a rare individual.

Here are some interesting statistics to consider.

- According to a 2011 CDC study on health in the U.S., 69.2% of Americans ages 20 and older are either overweight or obese.
- According to the *Statistic Brain* based on numbers from the U.S. Census 2010, the Federal Reserve, and the IRS, the average American family has only $3,800 in savings and 50% of Americans do not have a retirement account.
- The average American, according to the Nielsen company, watches five hours of television a day (on TVs, computers and smart phones). That's 150 hours a month, which is two years of viewing for every ten years of life.

If you want to be *normal* in America, you'll be overweight, spend most of your free time watching TV, live paycheck to paycheck, and worry about how you'll survive when you no longer work. As I've matured, I've come to realize being normal is not a characteristic for which to aspire.

On the Trail Less Taken

My good friends Jon and Mara had a unique wedding. They had all fifty guests meet them at Yosemite National Park. They led the way as they hiked the trail to Half Dome. It involved a fifteen-mile round trip trek and 4,800 feet of elevation. Once at the top, with the attendees that made it, they were married. My husband and I were not able to attend their wedding, so we did the next best thing. On their first anniversary, we flew to California and did the hike. It's a beautiful trail with views of waterfalls, forest, and woodland creatures—and not the scary kind that live in South Park, Colorado.

The hike had its challenges. Parts of it are steep or rocky, and it sometimes felt like it might never end, as if I was stuck in the Twilight Zone of national parks. After hiking a distance more than 39,000 feet, we came to the last 400 feet to the summit. The last leg was the most fun for me, but others often describe it as the scariest. It depends on how you look at it, because that last part of the Half

Dome ascent are the steel cables on the east side face of the steep rock. Prior to the installation of the cables in 1919, only people with rock climbing gear and ability could reach the peak. After the cables were installed, hikers could get to the top with no more equipment than the special gloves worn to protect their hands from being torn by the metal ropes.

When we arrived at the beginning of the cables, there was a long line of hikers there and as many already on the steel ropes. The cables are designed so climbers can hold on to the cable on the right to pull themselves up the rock face and hold on to the cable on the left to go down, which is actually on their right again when they are heading down. So there were two single-file lines heading in opposite directions stuffed between the parallel cables. The people ascending at the time we arrived were moving at the congested rate of a traffic jam during rush hour in the midst of a car accident on a strip of road undergoing construction. My hiking buddies have many positive qualities, but the patience to wait in a line like that isn't one of them, and they are definitely not normal people.

It only took a few minutes for them to decide on a faster plan of action. While all other hikers were content to wait in line for the safety that comes with doing the climb the way it was intended, we did a limbo-like bend under the right cable and began climbing the rock on the outside of the steel equipment. I was careful to only move my hand from one spot on the cable to another when my feet felt securely planted. The rock was a bit slippery, and on occasion, my shoe would lose its grip. There were wooden planks installed between the cables to assist hikers by giving them something to step onto during their ascent, which, of course, we didn't use since we were climbing outside of that set up. So I made sure I had a minimum of two spots of secure hold, at least a foot and a hand or two hands, before making any movements. I also made sure to say "hello" and "excuse me" to the people on the cables as I passed them and gripped the steel between their hands, since they were holding the same lines from the inside that I clung to from the outside.

A few short minutes later, we joined the rest of the celebrating climbers on the peak. After wiping the sweat from our brows and taking photos to commemorate our achievement, we found a quiet spot to sit and take in the wonderful views while tearing into the snacks and water in our packs. Had we waited in the cluster of line holders in the safer and easier section of the cables, we would have had much less time to enjoy the peak before needing to begin our descent. It was beneficial to be out of the norm in that situation.

Being different just for the sake of being different is not the message here. However, doing things a certain way, even if it's not in line with who you really are what you believe, just to fit in with the average is absolutely what I'm arguing against. When working toward a goal, sometimes it is necessary to work outside of the typical means in order to realize success.

The student who attends every class, works on each project ahead of time, rather than the day before it's due, and takes advantage of a professor's office hours or other resources designed to assist in academic success is every administrator's dream, because it's not as common as it should be. The twenty-year-old that begins investing for his retirement while his friends are driving more expensive cars and going out multiple nights a week is abnormal.

The mother who spends the few free hours she has, after taking care of her kids, her home and her job, taking on-line courses or other self-improvement programs, forgoing TV, is not ordinary. The health-focused restaurant goer that avoids the deep-fried goods, the entrees that are 90% meat and carbs, and the dessert menu, and instead chooses a more nutritious menu item is uncommon. For goals pertaining to wealth, professional or personal growth and health, doing what is common rarely ends up in success.

If I had done what was customary in my family, I would likely not have a high school diploma, I'd be burning through cigarettes while my junker of a car burned through fuel, I'd most likely have multiple children by various men, and I'd still be living in a trailer complaining about how cold it is during winter and hot during summer while paying high energy bills. In addition, my daily focus would be on which TV shows I'd watch at night, how I was going to pay the bills that month, and from which government programs I could get some free money.

Aaron's Story—Being Different and its Advantages

One of the best examples I know of standing out having a positive impact on a person's success is one shared by my friend and former mentee Aaron Ball. For third through tenth grade, Aaron was homeschooled. For his last two years, his mom worked at a small school whose mission was to help despondent—what some called hopeless—youths, and she enrolled Aaron there as well, since she would no longer be educating him at home.

Aaron joined a class of kids who were there as a last resort. They had been rejected or expelled from other schools or reassigned by their juvenile halls. Aaron recalls it being the first time he was exposed to conversations with other kids about sex, drugs, and drinking. "It was definitely a shock to the system," he said. "But I was self-aware enough to know I was pretty sheltered, and it was okay to be different while being friends with the other kids."

Aaron also went to a film program two hours each day for his last semester of senior year. He was admittedly not the most talented kid in class but still used it effectively to achieve his goals. He earned his first video production job working with a school for special needs kids when he was seventeen. "That job gave me a lot of confidence going into college," Aaron said.

When he began his freshman year of college, he was recruited for a student job by the school's TV studio. He took the position, beating out juniors and seniors who applied for it. Since he felt his videographer skills were well developed, he decided to major in Organizational and Interpersonal Communication so he'd develop another skillset. He figured having two areas of expertise would help him stand out more than having just one.

Aaron also auditioned for an international touring group to be their pianist. They would visit other countries during the summer and give concerts. Aaron explained to me, "I knew I wasn't as good technically as some of the others auditioning, but I felt like I had other qualities they'd want: personality, a team oriented attitude, and a strong work ethic." After auditions, the group leader told him he did not earn the position of pianist, but they liked him and wondered what else he could do. Aaron said he could operate the sound system, so they took him on as the only sound technician on the tour. After being beaten out by someone with a higher skill level at the audition, Aaron still got a position by standing out in other ways.

My final and favorite example was the day Aaron was invited to join a meeting with one of the influential men in his city. After college, Aaron had great experiences while figuring out what he wanted to do long term. He started his own business and sold it for six figures. He took a job with a cruise line to be their videographer and traveled the world for a couple of years. Then he started a new business, Ball Communications Group, which he currently owns. He continues to stand out from the crowd by being knowledgeable and current in his field, so he was invited by the general manager of a TV station to a group discussion off camera.

Aaron didn't know, going into the meeting, who would be in attendance. Once there, he realized Fred Levin was one of the twenty people in the room. Fred is one of his city's most successful, wealthiest and philanthropic citizens, deemed one of the nation's most successful civil trial lawyers by the Associated Press. University of Florida's law school is named after him.

During the meeting, Aaron watched as Fred spoke of a list of needed changes and how the eighteen other people in the room just nodded and agreed with whatever this influential man had to say. So when Fred finished speaking, Aaron introduced himself and spent the next twenty minutes asking Fred questions that would challenge his ideas with regards to the changes he had just proposed.

The meeting didn't impact Aaron immediately, but standing out as the one person willing to bring something different to that meeting, rather than being a "yes man" like the rest, made Aaron memorable which would help him later. Three months after the meeting, Aaron reached out to Fred by calling his office and asking to grab a coffee. Fred remembered him from the meeting and agreed to meet, all the while trying to figure out how to give him a few minutes and then let him down easily—something Fred mentioned when speaking about the experience.

Aaron, once again, made a great impression on Fred. One week after that meeting, Fred flew Aaron to Las Vegas for a meeting with a group of professionals, and then made Aaron their strategic analyst. Their business together has continued to grow since.

Standing out from the crowd has made a difference in Aaron's success at each stage of his life. Aaron said, "Early in the job market, you're usually poor. You are poor in experience, poor in perspective, and often poor financially. It helps to focus on people who can impact your needs. Spend time talking with them about their needs. When you can offer something that will help them, it often ends up helping you as well. Do that and you will definitely stand out."

If you are implementing concepts from this book such as positively affecting others, commissioning mentors to help you grow more quickly and acting in spite of fears, you will stand out. Without question, those strategies will impact your personal development and your resume. Those types of behaviors and choices will earn you a spot above the line of average.

Create a plan for success and take action even if it is uncommon. Stand out. Originality may earn you the position, promotion, or opportunity you seek. That's more likely to work than blending in with your competition. A great example of this is Kyle Clarke's post-college job search strategy. Rather than taking part in a typical job search—filling out hundreds of applications—he decided to create a website to advertise himself to employers all around the globe. The site was EmployKyle.com. Kyle said, "I decided I needed to come up with something that really made me stand out and so the idea to auction myself online grew." And it worked. He landed fifteen offers and accepted his dream job.

Be authentic. Being who you are is a precursor for happiness. Not being authentic just so you can assimilate will obliterate your joy and purpose. The confidence to be yourself is more magnetic than any other quality you could portray without 100% authenticity.

When you have something worthy to add, express it. If it makes you uncomfortable to be in the spotlight or because you worry no one will agree with your view, do it anyway. No one gets agreement from others 100% of the time, but staying silent will always remove the possibility of getting agreement from others as well as your chance to make a difference.

Once you've decided to distinguish yourself from others, one of the ways to do so is in your behavior choices. You'll do things others don't, so you'll get opportunities that others won't. While we are on the subject of standing out, let's talk about the type of communication that can put you miles ahead. You'll read about that in next chapter.

Gone In 600 Seconds

You can use the description you made at the end of the Chapter 9 or create a new list of positive words that describe you (personality and skill related).

Look over your identity description or descriptive list and underline any characteristics you've held back or kept hidden in order to blend in. Then decide if any of them are characteristics you want to let shine from now on.

MOST COMMUNICATION IS SELF-TALK

Chapter 14

Who is the person you communicate with the most? I ask because it's important whoever that person is feeds your mind with empowering thoughts rather than ideas that nourish your doubts, fears or insecurities. The most successful and most confident people still feel insecure from time to time.

We all do.

The key is in the ratio. You want to have more confidence than doubt, more things you like about yourself than things you dislike, and more positive thoughts than negative. To keep that ratio in your favor, it helps if the person whom you communicate with the most is providing the good more than the bad.

Internal Communication—We All Do It

Have you ever had someone ask you if you're talking to yourself? It's normal for our immediate answer to be something like, "Of course not. I'm not crazy."

What is fascinating is everyone talks to themselves. We all do; it just doesn't usually involve our vocal cords. In fact, we talk to ourselves internally more than we speak aloud to anyone else, and still, for as long as I can remember, people comment on it as if it's abnormal

Some experts believe all communication begins as intrapersonal communication, defined as communication for which the sender and receiver are the same person. Many of us don't realize we are doing it, but each thought that passes through our minds is a form of self-talk. If someone tells you to think of a cow, and you picture a brown cow, you told yourself cows are brown. You could have pictured a black cow or a black and white cow. If someone told you to think of a purple cow, you'd probably tell yourself there is no such thing.

To understand the significance of self-talk, we must also know the power of our subconscious mind. We have thoughts in our conscious mind, which we can call "on the surface". They are the ones we usually know we are thinking. We also have thoughts in our subconscious or "below the surface" that we don't actively recognize are there.

Here's one example that happens to me often, and I bet you can relate. Have you ever been trying to think of an actor's name or the name of a song and it just doesn't come to you? So you move on with your day and stop actively pursuing the answer. Then minutes or hours later, seemingly out of nowhere, it pops into your head? The reason is while your conscious mind ceased its hunt for the answer, your subconscious mind continued processing. Once it found what it was looking for, it fed the answer to your conscious mind.

Your conscious mind is the computer screen and your subconscious mind is the computer that stores information and continues processing in the background even when the screen is not showing what's happening. Understand this concept and you can easily recognize why self-talk is crucial to your success and fulfillment.

Internal Dialog Can Make or Break You

When I was a teenager, to say I struggled with negative thoughts would be a major understatement. I didn't pick out a single piece of clothing without evaluating the negative attention it could bring me. My internal dialogue went something like this: "What if I look stupid?" "Does it make me look fat?" "Will they know it's a hand-me-down?" "I hate my clothes." I also fretted about others' opinions on my hair, my pale skin, and the car I'd be seen in.

My senior year, I played on the school tennis team. My doubles partner, Amy, and I went undefeated the entire season and made it to the third round of the annual tournament. That's when things took a turn. I hit a couple of bad shots, and from then on the other team aimed every ball in my direction. They had found the weak link and they exploited it. Amy and I were evenly matched in skillset, but to her detriment, I was underdeveloped in mindset. When it became clear our opponents perceived me as the weaker player, it was enough to destroy my game. It is safe to say I hit errors on ninety percent of the balls that came to me from then on, and that is when our tournament play ended.

I remember crying. I remember Coach Gore attempting to calm me, his words falling on deaf ears. I remember running into Amy for the first time since that match, five years later, and my first words were, "I'm sorry for that match." All of these years later, I still recall clearly how my mind, during that match, was looping, "Why are they doing this to me? It's so unfair. Why am I sucking?"

I choked.

We lost.

It wasn't until years later I was taught the concept of asking myself the right questions, and the effect it has on my outcomes.

Let's say you are a professional whose work involves generating new clients. If a time arrives when you feel your prospects stagnate, you may ask yourself, "Why am I not getting new clients?" That would not be a productive question to send to your subconscious. Remember, it will continue processing that request. It may come back to you with answers like, "Because you are not good at your job," or "Because you don't deserve it," or "Because you are lazy or don't work hard enough."

To get a useful response that isn't going to make you feel like a loser, it is necessary to ask a useful question. So instead of "Why am I not getting any clients?" think something like, "How can I generate more interest?" Or, "What would be some creative ways to gain new prospects?" Even if the answers don't come to you immediately, your mind will continue processing. When it finds or notices suitable content, it will send it to the surface. If you've ever had a great idea pop into your head, it's probably because you asked yourself a great question whether or not you realized it. Tony Robbins said, "Successful people ask better questions."

Examples of how to choose a better question:

Not good: Why do I eat so much junk?
Good: How do I create a craving for good, healthy foods?
Not good: Why do I mess up on every test?
Good: How do I become a better test taker?
Not good: Why do we fight so much?
Good: In what ways could we communicate more effectively?

Negative self-talk lost me the tennis match, and years later, I had an even more challenging situation to deal with. Would I make the same mistake again?

Coaching Myself While Fighting for My Life

When I was 22, I took a business trip, which happened to be on a cruise. It was my first time on a ship. It was also one of my first times traveling as an adult and the first time I really experienced the power of this technique.

One of the ports was a private island that offered many activities including snorkeling. I had never been snorkeling so it seemed like a great opportunity to try something new. I was given a mask and breathing tube and declined the fins because they felt strange, made it difficult to walk, and I wasn't confident in my ability to paddle in them.

Two other young ladies and I jumped in the ocean with abandon and excitement. The first couple of times my head was under water and I could still see and breathe, I couldn't help but smile. It was a new and amazing world. Of course, the smile would break the seal between my skin and my mask, the mask would fill with water, and I'd have to stand up and readjust my equipment. By the third time under water, I was able to control my delight and my mask stopped flooding.

Once we were bored with swimming in circles near the beach, we headed out to deeper waters. I was surprised at how easy it was. We swam past the pier and turned so we were heading parallel to the beach. About fifteen minutes later, the other two girls were ready to head in, so I bid them farewell as I was eager to continue my exploration of the underwater world. Another ten minutes after that, I chose to turn around, knowing we'd be heading back to the ship soon.

That is when I encountered my first salt water challenge. I hadn't realized I was swimming with the current previous to turning around. However, when I turned to head back, it was unmistakable that I was swimming against it. I paddled my legs forcefully and my progress was nil, and when I popped my head up to take stock of my situation, I noticed the shore line on this side of the pier was decorated with huge, jagged boulders and during the short time I spent viewing that, the waves had pushed me closer to them.

So my state of affairs was this: I was swimming against a current, and I couldn't take breaks no matter my level of fatigue, because the current would drag me back and the waves would push me toward the dangerous rocks. I was alone and far from earshot of anyone else. I was on my own. *(Snorkeling lesson 1: always swim with a buddy.)*

Now you might be thinking, "Is she really sharing a snorkeling story? I mean, small children can snorkel, right? How intense could it be?" If I hadn't experienced this situation first-hand, I'd be inclined to follow your logic. The issue on this day was the current. It was the first I'd been in. According to reports on ocean drowning, the challenge for swimmers is spotting the current, and death is usually a result of exhaustion from fighting it. In April 2012, ocean currents caused the death of a fourteen-year-old boy at the Gulf Shores of Alabama and in June that same year, a woman caught in a current near Tampa, Florida died as well.

So there I was in my own current event, and after taking stock of my predicament, I put my head back in the water and paddled my legs and arms fiercely. This battle persisted for about 20 minutes, at which point my heart was attempting to jump out of my chest, my lungs were burning, and my vision experienced anomalies including spots floating in my vision field and shimmering zigzag patterns at the edges. It probably isn't necessary to tell you this, but I will anyway—I was a bit freaked. It was the first time I remember thinking I may not survive something.

In years past, I would have probably thought it was hopeless and given up. I may have panicked and made the physical challenge even tougher. I might have run through the disempowering thoughts available to me at that moment such as, "Those other girls shouldn't have left me out here alone," and "I have never been that great of a swimmer," and "I probably won't make it back in time and the ship will leave without me." Fortunately, I had already learned, when in any kind of situation that really challenges you, talking to yourself in a negative manner is a detriment and a waste of time and energy.

It was then that I pulled out my self-talk toolkit, and here's how the conversation went.

"You can do this.
You are going to make it.
You are a strong person.
Keep pushing.
You are almost there.
Control your breathing. In deeeeeeeply and out compleeeeeeetely.
Get the most out of every stroke.
Reach and kick.
You can do it."

I focused on repeating that thought pattern rather than on my burning muscles, and eventually, I rounded the pier and headed to shore. I hit the beach, literally.

When I dragged myself out of the water, I collapsed on the sand and lay there shaking with my chest heaving. Every limb was quivering from the strain, and at that moment, I didn't care how crazy I must have looked to everyone on the beach, if my bikini was positioned suitably, or if I was getting sand in my wet, matted hair. Instead I was grateful to be alive and to be finished with that particular challenge. Shortly after I stumbled onto the shore, the other two girls greeted me with tales of the difficulty they faced when they headed back, how they were worried about me, and how I should have taken the fins as they did, because it made the task a little easier. *(Snorkeling lesson 2: fins good.)*

Have you ever been to a sporting event where you cheered someone on? Do you cheer yourself on that way? The next time you find yourself in a challenging situation, try talking to yourself in an encouraging language and see how it makes you feel. It may sound silly to purposefully talk to yourself in this manner, but once you see the results, I think you'll find it isn't silly at all.

A Written Record of Your Thoughts

We all have constant internal dialog, and the words we choose are more powerful than most people realize. In addition to being aware of it, choosing empowering words and asking better questions, it helps to keep a written record. Most people call it journaling.

Keeping a written journal of your internal dialogue can be beneficial in a number of ways. It allows you to observe your own thought patterns. It provides an outlet for thoughts, which can provide peace to the user when she encounters a racing mind. I've seen that process called mind dumping—getting it out on paper so the brain lets go of the looping thoughts and allows the thinker to calm. Journaling also provides a location for ideas, thoughts, or epiphanies you want to revisit that could get lost if memory alone is relied upon.

One other value to journaling I've experienced is it provides a growth measure. Specifically, if you write down your goals or dreams, both short and long term, you can revisit the entries at a future date and experience the elation of progress. Imagine how it feels to jot down something as simple as wanting to learn a new skill and reading that entry thirty days, six months, or a year later once you've acquired it. It is an effective way to build self worth. Without the journal, it is easy for milestones to get missed in the continuity of passing time. A journal entry provides a snapshot of past thought, which you can compare to current mindset, therefore providing a measurement. It's similar to marking your height on the wall and standing next to it later in awe of your growth spurt.

Remember, you will talk to yourself (verbally or with thoughts alone) whether you want to or not. The decisions you'll have are in the words you'll use. Luckily, it is a simple success principle to implement. Robert Stuberg, one of the world's leading authorities on personal and professional success, talks about how important your thoughts are to your success. He says, "The most important relationship in your life is the one you have with yourself. And if you let those negative thoughts affect how you think, feel and act, how can you expect to build healthy relationships with anyone else?"

He goes on to say, "All too often, we reserve our harshest criticisms and our most negative thoughts for ourselves, and that is precisely what stands in the way of achievement."

To reach your Destination Awesome, continue asking yourself the right questions in the midst of challenging circumstances, remember how empowering thoughts helped save me as I fought against the power of the sea, and keep reading. The inspirational messages others share in these pages are here to serve as a reminder of the command you have over your own success.

Be aware of the self-talk you currently experience and work to improve it. What sort of questions do you ask yourself now and how can you ask better questions? If you still aren't convinced you are like the rest of us who talk to ourselves, set a timer for fifteen minutes and don't think at all until time is up. Unless you are a meditation guru, you'll probably find like the rest of us, it is difficult to stop the track meet of thoughts running through your brain.

Keep a journal. There isn't a correct way to do it or a certain platform you have to use. Keep it on your hard drive, online, in a notebook, in your daily planner, on your phone, iPad or tablet, or in an expensive, leather-bound book. The key is to keep one, not the type you keep.

Positive inputs are important. With or without your consent, you are bombarded daily with stimuli fighting for their place in your head. Much of it is not positive. They can be negative stories in the news, negative influencers in your life—the naysayers or Debbie Downers—or seeing things that cause an emotional reaction. Does seeing a homeless person on the street affect you?

When I see a homeless person, I feel pity for them and it makes me sad. It also makes me think about the economy and fret over whether that could ever happen to me. Though much of what you take in may be involuntary, it's up to you to choose to counteract the negative inputs with positive ones. You can read a story about an ordinary person making an extraordinary impact on the world like five-year-old Hannah Taylor. She started The Ladybug Foundation to help feed homeless people. Watch a cute YouTube video, view art that astonishes you, listen to a TED talk, laugh with your friends, cuddle a loved one, or attend a seminar designed to help you succeed in whatever endeavor you choose.

The more you can provide thoughts of a positive nature to your conscious mind, the higher the level of positivity that will transfer to your subconscious mind. You fill your vehicle's gas tank with fuel. You fill your stomach (your physical energy tank) with food. In the same pursuit of useful reserves, fill your mental tank with constructive information. So keep talking to yourself and make sure it's a quality conversation.

The communication you have with yourself is constant and takes deliberateness to regulate, making sure it's empowering. A similar concept—our focus—is what determines our mood and emotions. Find out how to wear your intention lenses and see with the right focus while on the Boulevard of Behavior.

Gone In 600 Seconds

Make a list of all of the positive inputs you will use to direct your mind toward empowering thoughts. Feel free to use some or all the ones listed above. For more ideas, you can also visit http://amieemueller.com/constructive-inputs-will-feed-your-brain/

Then put each of them in your calendar. I recommend doing them daily. You don't have to do all of them each day, but doing one or some of them every day is ideal if you can swing it. If not, use them as often as possible, so you have consistent positive inputs. Turn to the *Destination Awesome Action Guide* for more exercises and insight about cultivating empowering thoughts.

Chapter 15

REFRAME YOUR FOCUS

D o you ever feel a way you don't want to feel, and you can't explain why you feel that way? And you don't know how to change it?

Some days you may feel a little bummed even though nothing sad has occurred. Some days you may feel irritable even though nothing has happened to give you reason to be cranky. We have enough adversity in our lives causing the expected-to-follow negative emotions. We don't need those feelings plaguing us on neutral days too. This chapter covers the most helpful tool in fighting those negative emotions, no matter what their source, and it has nothing to do with dollar pitcher night.

Gaylene is a good friend of mine. She and I were both running sales and marketing businesses at the same time and we confided in each other both personally and professionally. Gaylene stood in my wedding and was one of the women I consistently went to for feedback. She is caring, smart, and a hard worker.

Gaylene once said to me, "Being around you taught me that no matter what the age, you can be young. You also taught me to laugh through hard things. When people were being difficult or things were going wrong, you laughed. I saw you ticked off, but still laughing. Crappy things happened and you still laughed—hitting a deer with your car, blood everywhere, car washes… still laughing."

No matter what is going on, you can choose your focus, and therefore, your feelings related to it.

Focus—A Force Stronger than Love

I fell in love for the first time when I was a freshman in high school. His name was Greer, and he was two grades ahead of me in school. The administrators let Greer and his friends start a short-term, after-school dance club. After the announcement was made, I and about twenty other students, showed up to a small classroom to learn some dance moves. Though I had never met him before, it took less than thirty minutes for me to become enamored.

From then on, I made an effort to find out where he'd be, and I'd show up there. I'm not sure what I expected from those *coincidental* run-ins, because I was still so shy that anytime he looked at me, I'd look away. A room of people laughed when Greer noticed my behavior and positioned himself in front of me again and again just to see me turn another direction. I liked him so much I couldn't bear for him to look at me, because I thought he'd see right through me. Still, wherever he was, I would go.

After a few months, we became friends. I wanted more, of course, but I'd take what I could get. Then after a few more months of hanging out in groups, he finally asked me out. During our time as a couple, one of the sweetest things he did for me was write me a letter almost every day. He had a study hall early in the school day, so he'd use that time to write me a one-page note, which he'd give to me between classes when we met at my locker. Those notes became something I looked forward to every morning.

Recently, years after Greer and I fell in and out of love, while cleaning out my closet, I found the pile of love notes. I enjoyed the nostalgia as I sat down and read through them.

The interesting pattern I noticed was how nearly every note mentioned the same thing. At least 80% of them said, "I'm not sure why you're mad at me," or "I wish I knew why you are in a bad mood." It amazes me how strongly

I recollect caring for that boy and yet even the most intense affection wasn't enough to extinguish the flames of my anger or bitterness back then. My *mood* was obviously noticeable. My focus on the aspects missing from my life—my unfavorable circumstances—put a strain on my relationships by blocking any sort of joy or feelings of contentment.

The dictionary defines focus as selectively concentrating on one aspect of the environment while ignoring other things. That's a perfect definition because there are three important keys to focus.

1. Select what you will focus on.
2. Concentrate on what you've selected.
3. Ignore things outside of what you've selected.

While dating Greer, I selected to focus on my poor circumstances. At the time, I didn't know I was choosing that focus, but in hindsight, it is clearly true. I concentrated on all I didn't have and I ignored the joy he brought to my life and the opportunities, since he opened up a whole new social group to me. If I had been knowledgeable then on the power of focus, I would have chosen to focus on my relationship with him and my good friends, and I would have ignored the temporary nonsense going on in my home life. With that focus, my circumstances wouldn't have been different, but my level of happiness would have.

I wasn't the sharpest pencil in the box when it came to having an empowering focus as a teenager, but there are many other teens and young adults who have experienced the power of a positive focus.

Waseem's Story—Without a Home but Not Without a Focus

Waseem spent his early childhood in Pakistan with his godmother while his parents satisfied the legal requirements that would allow them to bring him to the United States. When he was six, they brought him to New York to live with them in their basement apartment in Brooklyn. While building toward their American Dream, his father drove limos and his mother worked at a corner store.

While his parents were at work, it was up to Waseem to take care of his brother, Saif, who was two years his elder and handicapped. Saif's condition involved blood clots in his brain that inhibited normal mental development. Waseem would give Saif water and keep him company so he wouldn't get anxious. "It was sort of like he was an overgrown infant," Waseem explained. "He couldn't walk or talk normally."

While in middle school, Waseem's father started his own business and did very well. Waseem's world changed. They moved to a house on Long Island where Waseem had his own room for the first time, and his mom was able to stop working and be home with her two sons. Waseem said, "My parents never made us feel poor when we lived in the basement apartment, but when we moved, I could tell my parents were happier."

When he was fourteen, his world took a dramatic shift again. Waseem's dad got sick and needed a kidney transplant. The list of people waiting for kidneys in the U.S. was long, and they had a family member in Pakistan that was a transplant match, so the family traveled back to Pakistan. His dad had the surgery and started to improve but his immune system was weak. He got the flu and passed away when Waseem was fifteen.

After his father's death, Waseem and his mom were often at odds, his grades were slipping, and school was expensive in Pakistan, so when his uncle offered him a place to stay with him and his wife in Texas, Waseem accepted. Unfortunately, his aunt and uncle grew up in a different family culture than Waseem, and they clashed enough that Waseem moved out when he was sixteen. From that point on, he was on his own.

For the next two years, Waseem juggled classes, varsity football (and being the captain of the team his senior year), two part-time jobs, and a social life all while living in the minivan his parents left in the U.S. when they went to Pakistan. During the school year, his schedule was: 6AM to 5PM—school and sports, 6PM to 10PM—working at the YMCA, and 11PM to 4AM—working at a grocery store. During the summer, he took on a third job in construction to replace the school hours. The work he did wasn't only to support himself. He also sent money home to Pakistan each week to help support his mom and brother.

After two years of a grueling existence, he graduated high school, took a position with Vector Marketing, and began learning a new set of professional skills. Today, Waseem is a business owner. Within four months of founding his company, he had more money saved than ever before. He earns a good income, helps young professionals succeed and build their own business skills, and works in an environment of achievers, as he puts it. He's 22-years-old, debt free, in a happy relationship, and recently sent his mom the biggest check to date. He said it felt great to finally be able to provide more for his family.

I asked Waseem how he was able to pull it all off. Did he ever think of dropping out of high school? Did he ever consider giving up? Waseem said, "I wasn't totally alone. I had good friends in school and once in a while I'd stay at their houses for a night or two. I never stayed long because I didn't want to mooch off anyone. I had great teachers and a good school environment that really felt like my home at that time. Also, my department head at the YMCA found out about my situation and allowed me to use the showers and laundry facilities on site, which was a big help."

He continued, "Mostly I just did it. I never even thought about dropping out of school. I knew I needed to get school done. Sure, there were times I fell asleep in class or missed a practice, but my dad always taught me to do my best so that is what I did. Plus my mom needed money, so giving up was never an option."

I asked him how he managed the toughest days. He said, "I just focused on the positive outcomes that needed to happen, not the challenges. The same way in my current business, I don't focus on how unprepared I feel at times or beating myself up for mistakes. Instead, I focus on my strengths and making it a fun environment for the people who work with me."

So Waseem selected what to focus on: finishing school, how great he felt when with his friends and school family, and helping his mom and brother financially. He concentrated on those things and ignored the rest. He didn't sit around thinking about how hard it was, how many hours he worked, or how lacking his living quarters were in the van. He didn't focus on his losses; he focused on his future and what he could do in the present to ensure it was the future he wanted for himself.

Focus Changes Our Experience

Tony Robbins speaks of focus as being one of the major skills needed in order to be in an empowering state of mind.

I started feeling joy and fulfillment when I learned the importance of focus. Had I known how important it was while I was in high school, I could have easily concentrated on having a great boyfriend I was crazy about, the high grades I was earning, and the independence I had that is uncommon for teenagers. If I had, I could have been the girl voted "Most likely to be happy" in the yearbook. Instead, in a class of less than 140, I wasn't even mentioned in the voting of nearly 50 topics. Back then I spent most of my time focused on the unfairness of life, my disappointing family, and my lack of both money and popularity. Considering all of that, I am grateful I wasn't voted most likely to be a grumpy old lady with 50 cats.

A Singular Focus

Our brains only focus on one thing at a time. I have tested it, and my conclusion is it's a valid statement. I was in a meeting once with eight executives of Vector Marketing's Southwest Region, and I saw an email pop into my inbox. My internal dialog was, "Should I read it or continue listening to the speaker?"

I convinced myself I could do both. "I'll just read it really fast while also paying attention to the region manager, and it'll be fine," was what I told myself. I read the email looked back up to the speaker, and realized I heard nothing for the last sixty seconds. That's when I closed my email and went back to focusing on the meeting.

The conscious brain is quick at switching between thoughts, but that doesn't change the fact that it still goes through them one at a time. The better you get at controlling which thought is at the surface, the more control you'll have on your effectiveness. Whenever you feel yourself in a negative state such as frustration, anger, sadness, doubt, or fear, replace your focus with something more positive such as gratitude, respect, curiosity, confidence, or joy.

Turn frustration into curiosity by asking yourself what are alternative strategies or what you can learn from the current challenge. Turn doubt into confidence by remembering your past accomplishments. Turn anger into gratitude by thinking of all of the things you can appreciate about your life. Turn sadness into joy by remembering people or experiences that make you laugh.

To make progress toward your chosen destination, it helps to be in an empowering state of mind. Focus on the positive and the impact will be immense.

Vehicles to Take You to
AWESOME

Ask yourself, "Which negative emotions do I find myself experiencing most often?" and answer honestly. Recognizing what needs changing is the first step in any growth. Recognizing the moments you need a focus shift is the first step in taking control of your state. Everyone experiences negative emotions. The most positive, optimistic people you know have problems and times when they find themselves in disempowering states. The difference between them and people who struggle to find fulfillment is in their ability to redirect their focus back to something positive. You'll want to select what to focus on rather than letting your circumstances decide that for you.

Create resources to utilize during tough times. Make lists of things that make you laugh, things you are proud of, and those you are grateful for. When you feel stuck or in a negative mindset, read through one or more of your lists. It will refocus your mind positively. If not created ahead of time, this can be done in the midst of a disempowering state, but it's easier to do upbeat brainstorming when in an optimistic or neutral mindset. In other words, creating them ahead of time is easier than in the moment.

You can also sit down with a long-time friend and ask her or him to help you reminisce of great memories. Your friend will probably think of things that don't come to you, and your list will grow. After you've taken the first step of selecting what to focus on, these resources will help you actually do that. Then you're ready for steps two and three: concentrating on what you've selected, which is also choosing to ignore other things.

Look for the lesson in any failure. It's really not a failure if you learn from it; it's a temporary setback and a point from which to start again.

With the right focus, achieving what you want and getting to your desired destination becomes a more likely outcome. Once you have a clear picture of where you are currently and where you want to arrive, you can map out a route between the two points. The right focus helps keep you from taking a wrong turn. It's like the GPS voice of your brain, so if you do get off track, having that focus will help your mind recalculate the route. It will also help you see how to put yourself in a winning position, a principle discussed in the next chapter.

Gone In 600 Seconds

Make a list of things that make you smile and/or laugh. Be specific. Write out the details of a particular, fond memory. Write down the titles of funny videos and phrases of funny jokes. Keep your list handy. You want it easily accessible. When you need a pick-me-up, read it and visit the on-line videos.

POSITION YOURSELF FOR VICTORY

Chapter 16

I f your favorite celebrity was coming to your area to pick undiscovered people to star in his new movie or video, and you found out when and where he was going to be and that he was going to choose people randomly, not based on talent or tryouts, where would you be when he arrived? My guess is you'd be at that place at that time. You might even be early, and probably you'd be trying to get to the front of the crowd. Right?

Just like people who wait in line to get the first products or tickets released, the people who sit by the door so they can be the first off the bus, the people who run through the amusement park to get to an earlier spot in the roller coaster line, it helps to position ourselves for what we want.

Does position matter? Heck yes! They wouldn't have athletes compete in pre-match heats to determine their placement in the pool or on the track, if positioning didn't matter.

Lack of Positioning Hinders Success

I've heard people speak of how much they'd love to win the lottery, but upon further investigation, I find out they don't buy lottery tickets. As unlikely as it is to win the lottery when you're buying tickets, it's downright impossible to win when you aren't. I can't claim to be untouched by this kind of foolishness, because the lottery scenario isn't completely unlike the cheerleading fantasy I had while I was in high school. I yearned to wear the cute uniform made of our school colors, red and baby blue, adorned with a capital L. I wanted to be a member of the Lakeland Laker cheer squad.

I aspired to be a cheerleader. I dreamed about it, thought about trying out when I'd see the posts on the school's walls, and attempted the cheer jumps in the concealment of my yard when no one else was around.

It wasn't the idea of popularity or the attention of boys that made it so desirable, though those would have been nice side effects. What I loved about it so much was that they were entrusted with the tasks of inspiring a crowd, bringing people of all types together on one common goal and using only positive encouragement in the process. It doesn't hurt that I am drawn to a group of people creating one simultaneous movement. To this day, I love to line dance, no matter how dorky it seems, because I love moving with a group. My favorite sport to watch on ESPN is the cheerleading competition because of both the group choreography and the stunts, and I love to see flash mobs and the dance routines on *So You Think You Can Dance*.

As I attempted those jumps in my yard, I was not good. I thought with coaching I could be, and I wanted it so badly. And that is where the road became a cul-de-sac. My cheerleading fantasies never progressed past wishing, and at the time, I thought it was because circumstances were stacked against me. I didn't have the money to buy the uniforms and proper shoes, I didn't have the training other girls had, and I wasn't born with the ideal body for it, so I was unlikely to prevail even if I tried out. All of those excuses were the pyramid atop the foundational detail that I didn't possess the confidence to go after what I desired.

In retrospect, there were many things I could have done to position myself to have a chance of being accepted to the squad. I could have asked one of the girls to tutor me in the stunts and routines before tryouts. I could have searched for books about the sport and increased my knowledge of it. I could have asked the coach to assess me and find areas of improvement. I could have swallowed my fears and tried out anyway, knowing if I didn't make it, I was no worse off. To have tried and failed is worthy of some praise, whereas to not have tried at all is pitiful.

Positioning Leads to Positive Results

What is the point in allocating mental energy to dreams if we're not willing to take even the smallest steps to increase the likelihood of them coming to fruition? I've learned, at the very least, you can put yourself in a position to have a shot at what you want, and I'm glad I did, because for me, it has made a difference. I was never a cheerleader, but positioning has assisted me in achieving many other goals.

After the first eight sessions of my Literary Analysis college class, it was clear who the professor believed was showing the greatest talent. Our homework was to read a story, analyze its meaning, and write a report. During each discussion of the previous assignment, our instructor would read the passages he enjoyed from the students' papers. Some of my classmates' works were never made public. I was cited on occasion, but the compositions of a young man named Marcus were shared most often.

A third of the way into the semester, our teacher announced we would pick partners to work with for the remaining weeks leading up to finals. Our companion would be whom we'd bounce ideas off and whom we'd provide with our assignments before turning them in, so that partner could proofread and make suggestions. He told us we'd pick our partners during our next class session.

Up to that time, I had sat in the back of the small room. I was still shy and timid; I didn't speak up in class or talk to my classmates. As soon as they announced we'd pick partners, my mind started working on plots to be paired with Marcus. The challenge would be joining him without actually asking him, since I did not have the confidence to vocalize any such proposition. The idea of rejection was too overwhelming. I hadn't yet started the sales job at that point, so I hadn't yet built up my resolve.

I did the only thing I could think of. I showed up early that day and parked myself in the second row of the classroom right next to the desk in which Marcus usually sat. I sat there hoping the musical chairs I would start by taking someone else's place would not end in Marcus' seat being occupied by another student. I was relieved when Marcus walked in and took his normal seat.

There I sat, wondering if I could work up the nerve to ask him to be my partner, understanding the anxiety people must feel when they consider asking others for a date. I avoided looking at him, and instead, fidgeted with my textbook. I sat there hoping that even though I had pulled my hair back, I wasn't accidentally showing off the bald spot that I tried so hard to keep hidden.

Halfway through the class, the professor announced the time had come to choose our mates. I turned my head toward Marcus, and as I did, he looked at me, did a little shrug of the shoulders, and asked, "Want to work together?"

I answered, "Sure" with as much indifference as I could muster, and that began our friendship. We received top grades, set the curve for the class, and continued to have our work read aloud by the professor for the rest of the semester. We were the power team of the class, and it started with my choice to position myself for what I wanted.

Positioning has proven its importance repeatedly throughout my life. When I took a sky diving class, the instructors repeated the importance of body position while falling at a rate of approximately 1,000 feet every 6 seconds. It wasn't clear to me how crucial it was until I jumped solo, without a tandem master, for the first time. Slight changes in body position create unexpected shifts while free falling, and proper body position is paramount for successful parachute deployment. Just as positioning myself for what I wanted to achieve in Literary Analysis, or while jumping out of a plane, positioning yourself for what you want will assist in achieving your goals.

Later in life, I made a choice to position myself for what I wanted, and again, it helped. While living in Tulsa, Oklahoma, I was interested in a career move with a company in Austin, Texas. After speaking with people at the Austin company, the situation was a position may open up but wasn't currently available. Knowing they'd want someone to fill it quickly if it came available, I decided I needed to live in Austin. I had worked my way up to a post with the company in Tulsa that allowed me to transfer to Austin and continue working with them. When the job I wanted in Austin opened up, I was able to give more than enough notice to my current employer and accept the new position. Already being in Austin gave me a leg up on the interviewing competition.

Whatever you aspire to, putting yourself in a position for it can be helpful. The ways you can position yourself include building skills, networking, making an impression on others, and your physical location. For example, if you're looking for work, why not use the hours before or after job searching to volunteer? Being an unpaid worker can provide opportunities to meet influential people who could make future job decisions or know of work available elsewhere. It could help you build skills in a new industry, which could increase your marketability and make a positive impression on decision makers. It would also get you out of the house, which is where the career opportunities will be.

Aiden's Story—From Addicted and Broke to Sober and Successful

Aiden is a business associate of mine whom I interviewed via conference call a few years ago because he was succeeding at an unusually high level in his company. He understands the power of positioning better than most. While Aiden was in college, he began using pain medicine as a recreational drug. His junior year, senior year and post graduation, he was using it for more than recreation. He was an addict.

He was a mostly functional addict. He still completed classes, still did okay at his sales job, and still had relationships with family and friends. His addiction gradually became more severe. It got to a point where he knew he needed to stop and kept telling himself he'd quit tomorrow or next week—days that would never come.

He said, "When you begin using, it seems like no big deal. It feels good, and there isn't much downside. The problem is when you keep doing it, you need to increase the dosage to get the same feeling, which is harder on you physically and financially. Eventually you get to the point where you are so dependent, you need to take it just to function."

Soon after college graduation, at the height of his addiction and usage, he ran out of money. All of his money had gone to pain meds and he was tapped out. "It was affecting me financially, but it was also affecting my relationships, my family, and my soul," Aiden said. "So I finally told my mom."

Aiden's mom was a recovered alcoholic. He figured she would understand what he was going through. She did, and she helped Aiden position himself for recovery. He moved home and began attending meetings for addicts. He had zero access to money; his mom managed all of his finances. When Aiden was given money, it was always in the form of a gift card so he could not spend it on drugs. He ceased all connection with friends and suppliers that supported his habit. He removed them from his phone, avoided areas they'd hang out, and didn't take any calls. He kept working. He found having something positive to dive into and focus on to be very helpful. And he got a sponsor, a mentor who had been through addiction and overcame it.

The system positioned Aiden for success for the next four months. Aiden describes withdrawal as the hardest thing he's ever had to contend with. He said it was totally worth it, though. Now, not only does Aiden help others with similar issues by speaking at drug addiction groups, but he has reached new and exciting heights in business as well. While using drugs and working over the summer breaks, Aiden's sales performance was under $80,000 for two summers combined. In sobriety, and in his early twenties, his next summer sales performance grew over 400% winning him the top sales performance in his region. The professional results of breaking his addiction were undeniable. His income grew dramatically, and he became a sought-after trainer and speaker within his company.

Positioning had its impact on my college success as well as my business, and Aiden would likely still be an addict had he not positioned himself for successful rehabilitation. When you look at the list you created of things you want to accomplish, consider how you can position yourself for success for each of them.

Position yourself with people. Network to know the people who can make a positive impact in your life. Who are the decision makers? Influencers? Experts? People who can counsel you? People who can cheer you on? Get to know them and let them get to know you.

Position yourself with capabilities. Build any skills or get educated on things that can help you in your endeavors. There are too many options to make excuses. You can read books and blogs, seek out a leader of any area, listen to instructional audios, take classes, apprentice, volunteer, attend a seminar, and watch videos on nearly any subject in which you desire to improve.

Position yourself in any moment, anywhere, by making a good impression. People scoff at first impressions having an impact, but disliking the judgmental aspect of it doesn't negate its validity. Initial impressions aren't the only ones you'll make, but they can set the tone, so make sure they are good. Whatever you're looking to achieve, the impression you give should be appropriate. Impressions are derived from a combination of your appearance, communication, and demeanor. Be confident, positive, attentive, and smile.

Position yourself physically. Your location can also have an impact on your success. If you want to work in a particular area, it will help if you are in or close to that area. At the very least, do the research to know about that area and how you could quickly set yourself up there, if needed. If you desire to meet someone, be in a place where you'll have that opportunity. To impact the people in your life, be where they are. To lose weight, don't locate yourself in fast food restaurants. In other words, don't play hide and seek with success. It finds you more easily when you are in its path.

You've probably heard someone say they were able to take advantage of an opportunity because they were in the right place at the right time. The problem with that statement is it makes it sound like happenstance. Usually it wasn't luck that put them in that place at that time but rather a series of choices or behaviors.

Boulevards are usually wider than common roads or paths and have multiple lanes on which one can choose to drive. On the Boulevard of Behavior, we all have seemingly infinite choices when it comes to our personal behaviors, so we must choose wisely. The next chapter will cover the final conduct on the Boulevard of Behavior that helped me escape a world of deprivation.

Gone In 600 Seconds

Make a list of three things you want to achieve (in any time frame) or refer to the list you made in Chapter 1. Then brainstorm ways to position yourself for those goals, such as people to meet who could help you or skills to develop.

It's never too early to start positioning yourself. Even if it's a two-year or three-year goal, you can start building skills and contacts now. Turn to the *Destination Awesome Action Guide* at the back of the book for more ideas about positioning yourself for success.

Chapter 17

DECIDE WHAT NEEDS TO BE SACRIFICED

W hen you decide to study, you are also deciding not to sleep, watch TV, or go out with friends. When you decide to make dinner, you are also deciding not to eat out, get take out, or be hungry. When you decide to watch a movie, you are also deciding not to watch a different movie. You get the point.

Every time you decide how to spend your time, you are also choosing how not to spend your time. Whether you realize it or not, you are constantly choosing what to sacrifice. In addition, the sacrifices will always outnumber what you choose. For example, choosing five classes for a semester means you're missing out on the other hundreds of classes offered that semester. That can make it seem like hundreds of sacrifices to five gains.

Anytime we choose something, we are not choosing countless others. Our perception of sacrifice can make us feel a heavier weight of loss than it actually is. We feel the weight of all things we did not choose when, to be fair, we would have only chosen one other, if our choice was different. We have to remind ourselves that our perception of sacrifice and how bad it feels is often overdramatized or overestimated.

Though our perception of loss can be adjusted through logic, the fact remains: we do have to make sacrifices. The question is are you making the most optimal choices and sacrifices, those that will lead you to your truest desired outcomes?

Indulgence Versus Sacrifice

My senior year of high school was probably the year that most plainly pointed out the financial differences between me and my classmates. That was the year of spending. My fellow students were getting senior pictures taken, ordering class rings, buying caps and gowns, taking senior trips, and sending application fees to multiple universities. Even on our tennis team, many girls were sporting new shoes, new athletic gear, and new tennis racquets. It was their last season and they wanted to look as good as they played.

I longed to have a shiny, new class ring. The vendors came to the school and handed out brochures touting all of our options: gold, silver, white gold, dainty bands, thick bands, and various stone shapes and colors. I had never worn jewelry, but I wanted a class ring so badly.

I would have also loved to have a nice tennis racquet. The one I was using was a hand-me-down from Lisa, which I so much appreciated, because you couldn't join the team without a racquet. But when she and I practiced outside of team hours, she would sometimes let me play with her newer, more expensive racquet. I didn't do that too often, though, because I didn't want to seem ungrateful for the one she gave me, and I didn't want to get too used to playing with a better racquet only to switch back when it was game day. That could have been bad for my game.

So I used the money I made working over the summer to buy the cheapest cap and gown I could find, because it was required to be part of graduation. I got a few senior pictures taken—the smallest package I could get. And I applied to only one school, because I didn't want to pay to apply at more.

I did not get a class ring, go on senior trips, or buy new sporting equipment. Those were things I could have used my savings for, but then affording to go to college would have gotten more difficult. That was the story of my teenage years—constantly choosing between things when it came to spending money. I couldn't afford everything I wanted, so I had to prioritize what I wanted most.

And I wanted to get out of that trailer park. I wanted to leave the town where everyone knew me as the poor, quiet girl and start fresh somewhere else. I wanted to create a more exciting and happier life, and to do that I had to make sacrifices.

As I got older, I came to realize learning to prioritize and to resist overindulging is a useful skill. Though I'm not an expert on all things financial, you don't have to be as money savvy as Donald Trump or Warren Buffett to recognize some basic mistakes made by people who struggle financially. There are people who earn a good income and still struggle based on their financial choices. It's not as much about the level of your pay as it is about what you do with your pay that determines financial success. Though earning a high pay is still preferable and something I recommend, it is not the sole or main variable to your financial freedom.

I feel bad for my family. Most of them still deal with wondering how they'll pay their bills some months, how they'll be able to afford gifts during the holidays, and what will happen when they can no longer work. I feel fortunate, because since I was eighteen, I've taken care of myself and my finances. I've never had a bill go unpaid, and by the time I was twenty-three, I had a great credit score. When I was twenty-eight, I bought my first house, which sold a few years later for a profit.

At this point, the mortgage on our current home is the only debt Josh and I have, and it will be paid off fifteen years early. In addition, we are grateful to be able to travel, invest in personal growth, and support multiple charitable organizations. I'm happy I've been able to help my parents financially when they've needed it and that I've learned enough regarding financial management to be in such a position.

Some people look at having money, or not having money, as something related to luck or opportunities only given to certain people born into particular socioeconomic levels. I was raised in the same environment as the rest of my family members who still have limited financial options. I went to the same public schools, and had the same opportunities. The reason I'm in a better place financially is because of the different choices I made as a young adult—namely the decision to sacrifice rather than indulge. Shauna Niequist, Author of *Bittersweet*, said, "It's not hard to decide what you want your life to be about.

What's hard is figuring out what you're willing to give up in order to do the things you really care about."

I decided early on I wanted more than the trailer park and living paycheck to paycheck. I wanted to stop being just an observer in the art of fulfillment. So even as a teenager, I limited my indulgences. I didn't indulge in sex, drugs, smoking, skipping school, or putting off the responsibilities of adulthood.

In Indiana, a person could work when they turned fourteen. I applied and interviewed for a job before my fourteenth birthday and started work the day after. I sacrificed a lot of fun, teenage time to be a wage earner and an A student.

After high school, I sacrificed the same things during college to maintain the same grades, support myself, pay for school, and graduate with a degree as quickly as possible. When I started my career, I lived in really inexpensive housing. People who cared about my well-being asked me if I was sure about living in the area I chose. They were thinking it was unsafe and I could get hurt. I was thinking it was cheap and I could save money. I also ate inexpensive groceries rather than restaurant food. There was a semester of college I survived on little more than PB&Js, mac-n-cheese, and canned ravioli. Granted, that is not a diet I'd recommend for someone who is health conscious, but it did fill my tummy for very little money.

I didn't really buy luxuries of any kind. I kept the same cell phone until it died rather than getting the latest version. I drove a fuel efficient, no frills car, and I only bought professional clothes when they were on sale. Many of my first suits came from thrift shops and friends who got them from women in their families.

I have the same temptations as others. I'd see the commercials for the latest gadgets or see other people on campus with them, and I'd think about how cool it would be to have them. I saw beautiful women with manicured nails and shiny, perfect hair I figured only the expensive hair products would produce. In those moments I'd sometimes feel bad because I didn't have those things. But then I'd get back to work, knowing the only way to have them was to earn them. I knew if I continued making the right choices and working toward my goals, some day I'd have those things too. And I wouldn't have to sacrifice my future plans or good judgment to get them.

Money wasn't the only sacrifice I made, though. As a young professional, I worked long hours. In my early adult years, what I majorly lacked in social skills, positive mindset, and confidence was made up for by my strength in discipline and sacrifice.

Indulgence seems to be one of the greatest enemies of success. Americans are overweight because we indulge in nutrient-poor foods and hours in front of the television. The nation's people are struggling financially because we indulge in immediate gratification even if it means we buy with credit or funds we don't really have. According to the U.S. Census Bureau, Statistical Abstract of the United States: 2012, more than 40% of births in this country are to unmarried women and of all countries on the report, the U.S. has the highest percentage of single parent households. It appears we also indulge in starting families before we are truly stable.

Sacrifice leads to greater long-term outcomes. Healthy people sacrifice free time to exercise and sacrifice tempting foods for a nutrition emphasis. Some sacrifice money to pay higher prices for organic or non-GMO foods. People on their way to wealth sacrifice immediate consumer gratification for saving and investing gains. Great parents sacrifice many things, not least of which is their own leisure time, for their children. Top students often sacrifice free time for extra studying. Superb athletes sacrifice their free time for additional practice. The list goes on and on.

Yasemin's Story—A Fourteen-year Sacrifice

Thankfully, most of us don't have to make as sizable or as long-term a sacrifice as Yasemin Inal had to make in order to pursue her dreams. Yasemin grew up in Istanbul, Turkey and in her last six years of school there, she learned English as her second language. One of her teachers encouraged her to go to America to attend higher education. The prospect of gaining a new experience, studying abroad, and meeting people from all over the world was enticing. So she went to the U.S. to attend Ohio University where she majored in Public Relations and Journalism.

When her freshman year wrapped up, she went home for the summer at her father's request. At the end of summer, her dad passed away. She lost him six days before her flight was scheduled to leave Istanbul. Feeling grief for her father and concern for her mother, Yasemin had a big decision to make. Would she go back to school in the U.S.—which she absolutely loved and where she felt she belonged—or would she stay so her mother wouldn't be alone? Yasemin was the youngest of three siblings and was the only one still at home.

Though Yasemin didn't know it, her father had a conversation with her mother right before he passed. He asked her to be strong and let Yasemin go. He asked his wife to be selfless and help Yasemin continue to work toward her own dreams. It was Yasemin's life to live, after all. So her mom encouraged Yasemin to make the decision without concern for taking care of her mother.

Yasemin decided to continue pursuing her dreams in America. When I spoke with her about this choice, she said, "Prior to getting on the plane, I was in pain, but I think I was still in shock. On the plane, his death really hit me. He was my best friend and the strongest figure in my life. I remember him telling me he didn't want me to ever rely on a man to take care of me. He wanted me to be able to take care of myself." She continued, "I cried the whole way from Istanbul to New York."

Besides the obvious loss, her father's death set in place a new set of challenges. He had been paying her college tuition bills, but that was no longer an option. Her mom would now only receive a small amount of money and when taking the exchange rate into account due to Istanbul's poor economy at the time, it would be next to nothing in U.S. dollars. So it was up to 17-year-old Yasemin to support herself for the first time.

Yasemin visited the international student office immediately to discuss her options. Being on a student visa limited her opportunities. She could only work on campus. So she needed to find work on campus that would pay enough and offer enough hours to cover tuition of $20,000 a year, and living expenses. After looking at the numbers, Yasemin realized one job wouldn't cut it. She worked three: she tutored women from other countries to help them learn English, she worked in the library, and she worked in the language lab. Over the years, she moved into other campus jobs, including being a resident assistant and campus safety.

"Some days I'd ask myself how I was ever going to make it," Yasemin said. "I definitely had moments of despair, especially early on, but little by little, I got back on my feet."

Yasemin finished school and graduated with honors. Today, she is a citizen of the U.S. and is happily married with three children. She is the CEO and founder of *Amplify Your Dreams* for which she does motivational speaking and personal development coaching.

When I asked Yasemin about the biggest sacrifices she had to make in order to succeed in such challenging circumstances, she said, "Leaving my mom behind was the biggest. She was super patient and would never complain when I'd call her. She'd tell me not to worry about her, that she was taking care of herself."

Not seeing her mom was a huge sacrifice for Yasemin. Not only did she not see her during the school year, but since she didn't have the money, she didn't see her during breaks either. "I spent my spring, summer, and winter breaks at school. I couldn't afford the plane ticket home."

Even after she graduated, and her student visa expired, Yasemin took on an internship, which qualified her to stay in the U.S., but didn't qualify her for international travel. Once she had a work visa and began applying for permanent residency, it became risky to leave the U.S. while waiting for approval. After 9/11, travel became even more restricted. Fourteen years passed before Yasemin saw her mother. "I just prayed she'd stay alive and healthy until the day I could see her again," Yasemin said.

It was clear, time with her mother was the biggest sacrifice she made. Still, I knew there had to be more she sacrificed during that time. Having three jobs and a full load of classes is not an easy undertaking, so I asked her to share more about her experience.

Yasemin explained, "Growing up, we were comfortable financially, and my dad was from a culture of family feasts. So I never thought I'd have to think about how I would buy something to eat. As a resident advisor, room and board was covered, which included one meal a day. So I'd eat dinner in the dining hall because it was the largest meal. Then I'd eat small things at all other times such as yogurt, fruits, and other snacks. Sometimes I'd go into the grocery store and see my favorites from childhood such as lamb and I'd dream about eating it. Before that, I never had to be frugal with food. It really taught me to budget, which is a skill that has come in handy in my life."

I'm sure if I had spoken with Yasemin while she was in college, I would have felt her sacrifices were a horrendous burden. I am astounded at all she had to deal with back then. However, when I speak with her now, I get the impression that everything she had to go through then was totally worth the life she has now. She loves her life, her family and her business. As you experience your own sacrifices, remember they are only temporary and usually lead to a more awesome fulfillment down the road.

Sacrifice Pays Off

Sacrifice is a permanent fixture in the life of a successful and growing person, but what is sacrificed is temporary in most cases. When I abstained from consumerism, it was to implement a strategy of developing savings and investments. Once I hit the minimum goal I had determined for myself, I was able to indulge in spending once in a while. I still classify myself as a frugal person, but I'm also able to splurge on occasion. Splurging now on massages, travel, and gifts for friends and family is much more rewarding than splurging on eating out, driving an expensive car, or having the latest cell phone would have been when I was younger.

An entrepreneur starting a business will sacrifice free time until it is built to a certain level. I worked seventy-hour weeks to build my business, but two years later, my staff was capable, and I was able to spend every Tuesday on the golf course with a friend rather than in my office. And as my staff took over more, removing things from my work plate, I paid them more. It was worth sacrificing some profit to make sure they felt appreciated.

As you think about which areas of your life you'd like to improve, you'll also need to think about what things you'll need to give up. Those things don't have to be a devastating loss, and your perspective will determine how you feel about them. Remember to reframe if you need to. You can look at your sacrifice with negative correlation or you can look at it as a step toward freedom; a step toward the life you want and your Destination Awesome.

At the end of previous chapters, you already decided where you want to go and created a plan. Now, **add to your plan both what you need to gain and what you need to sacrifice.** For example, for financial success, you might need to gain financial education and sacrifice unnecessary purchases.

Do not fall prey to the "there's nothing I can do about it" attitude. Regardless of your situation now, you can change it for the better. Jim Rohn said, "You cannot change your destination overnight, but you can change your direction overnight." Any step in the right direction will move you toward your goal, including any sacrifice for that direction, because it's proof your mindset is changing and growing.

You don't have to give up everything you enjoy or indulge in, however, you will need to **limit your indulgences.** The sacrifice should be the majority and the indulgence the minority. My husband and I are the healthiest we've ever been. We eat healthy and limit our desserts, but that doesn't mean we never partake in sugary treats. Once in a while, we enjoy cookies, dark chocolate bars, or coconut milk ice cream. It's just not a regular indulgence we allow ourselves. Instead we delight in feeling well and having energetic, lean bodies.

Gone In 600 Seconds

Think about the past three months. Is there anything you've done that you think should be on the sacrifice side of the T chart rather than the indulge side? If so, create a plan for changing that. Do you need to cut back on TV or video games? Cut back on spending or shopping? Cut back on the number of nights you go out? Cut back on indulging in negative emotions? Whatever it is, make a positive change and you'll get positive results.

Chapter 18   ALL PIECES OF THE PUZZLE

What could you accomplish if you put all of the concepts in this book to work for you? Each topic was laid out separately, but I'm sure you've noticed many of them fit together like pieces of the same puzzle. Finding the good and strengths in others and being open to learning from them has an impact on selecting an empowering peer group. Your self-talk will often fall in line with your focus. Your fear of rejection will decrease as the thickness of your skin increases. In addition, you'll be above average by taking action when you're scared, being productive with your time, and being disciplined in sacrifice in a time of overindulgence. Strengthening every skill listed here will position you for success.

Here's an example of multiple concepts coming together and how they impacted me and a group of people in an unsavory situation.

On a cold day in central Texas, a rare weather pattern, I drove from Austin to San Antonio for an event at one of the expo centers. As I approached the highway exit, minutes before the start of the event, traffic congested quickly. Vehicles were eager to get into the parking lot, whizzing left, right, and straight ahead. I followed a line of cars into the rear parking lot, figuring it would be faster to park and walk a good distance than to compete for a closer spot. Leaving my coat in the car, because I didn't want to hold on to it while inside, I happily hurried into the building.

Hours later, after doing my part to stimulate the economy via consumerism, I sauntered out to the parking lot. When I found my parking spot, my car was not in it, and a crowd of people stood nearby. They must have noticed the confusion displayed on my face, because they explained what happened. Nearly three hundred of us were the unwilling customers of one of the most efficient towing companies in San Antonio. I had not seen the small signs suggesting we not park in that lot when I pulled into the spot. However, once the cars were cleared away, the signs were visible, and I called the number displayed to begin the vehicle recovery process.

As the taxi dropped me off at the towing company, I joined a line of more than 50 people waiting for their turns to pay $300 to rescue their vehicles from impound. Apparently this towing company planned for all of the big events held at this expo center, knowing the back lot would be full and they would make a killing on those days. They even hired independent tow truck drivers to help so they could get more cars out before the people inside the expo heard about it and moved their vehicles out of the line of fire.

We stood in line for more than six hours. Only one person was allowed in the tow company's building at a time, and each person was inside for about ten minutes. Most people did not have coats since they weren't planning on spending much time outside that day. Food, drink, or any other comfort was nowhere to be found. It was a line filled with very unhappy people. It was as if all my years of training and the lessons I learned were being put to the test.

Being trusting. When I found out I had been towed, I went back inside the expo and talked to the vendor with whom I had spent more than $600. What I purchased was too heavy for me to carry so I couldn't take it with me to the towing location. I asked them to hold onto it. It was a company from more than 120 miles away and the vendor didn't know when I'd be able to get it from them next, but I had to trust they would get it to me somehow. I did get the product three months later when they were near my location again.

Positive self-talk and a good focus. As I stood in line, it grew longer behind me as more people left the expo and realized their cars were impounded. Waiting to retrieve my car and shivering, I thought of anything positive to take my focus off my suffering. I thought, "Soon I will be in my car with the heater on full blast, at least I'm not the last in line, and keep moving so your muscles generate heat." I spent a lot of time jumping and jogging in place.

Affecting others. Everyone in line was unhappy, especially the parents whose kids were standing outside shivering with them. When an older gentleman with white hair wearing a veteran's cap came out of the office clearly upset, he shared with everyone in line only cash was accepted and he was told to walk down the road to an ATM in order to pay to collect his car. He looked defeated. As he began to walk away, I assured him when he returned, he would go to the front of the line. He was surprised and looked for confirmation from the people in line ahead of me. When they agreed, his spirit was lifted a bit, and he left to make the trip on foot to the ATM.

I also talked a lot with the few people immediately in line ahead of and behind me. I asked them about themselves and what they enjoy. I made them laugh a few times. I was smiling and telling jokes. I think they thought I was strange. One of the men in front of me said, "You are way too happy to be here." It felt good to know I could bring a little light to a dark day.

When a cameraman from WOAI, one of the local news channels, showed up to record the state of affairs, my line-mates told me to get interviewed. So I did, along with the military vet when he returned with his cash, and a couple of the parents. According to other news reports, this towing company had been investigated before for shady business practices.

When my interview wrapped up, I persuaded the cameraman to give me a ride to buy coffee. He was nice enough to oblige me as well as a couple of ladies from the line who joined me. When we returned, I handed out more than forty coffees to people in line hoping it would help a little in their efforts to stay warm. It wasn't an expensive gesture, but made a bigger difference than you'd usually think $50 could make. One of the men in line offered to help me pay for them. I thanked him but asked him to keep his money. I love how kindness triggers more kindness. It made me feel good to positively affect many people that day.

Productivity during a down time. Since I hadn't planned on being in line for six hours when I started the day, I didn't have a book or any work with me. So the best I could do with some of that time was delete unnecessary photos from my phone to free up memory, brainstorm ideas for upcoming meetings, and call friends and family to catch up. Of course, being there gave me an interesting story to share.

If this experience happened to me years earlier when I was still an untrusting, angry-at-the-world, victim-minded, lacking-in-social-skills young adult convinced of my bad luck and the unfairness of life, I know I would have ranted about the unjustness of it all. I would have had a six-hour frown, a detrimental stress level, a focus on all things I would have preferred to spend $300 on, and would have done no one any good. I'm grateful to have grown into a person with a better concept of attitude and serving others. At the end of the day, I got my car back, drove home to meet my wonderful husband for the date I was hours late for, and anticipated seeing myself on the news.

It turned out our part of the broadcast was cancelled when a shooting occurred and took precedence. Oh well; the news would have only shown the negative side anyway. It would not have aired the way people tried to keep each other warm, lifted each other's spirits, or celebrated once they had their vehicles back. So viewers wouldn't have seen the magic within the adversity, and that was the real story of the day.

As I write the stories in this book about my family and childhood, I am concerned I'll upset those I care about by airing the dirty laundry for you to read. I've concluded if it makes a positive difference in your life—that you may read them, relate to them, and make a change that will lead to a higher level of happiness and fulfillment—then it is worth taking the personal risk of having to atone for my transparency.

I also want you to know that though I believe I've had the largest transformation, my loved ones are not without growth themselves. In an effort to provide to you well rounded, accumulated learning, I asked my family members to share the life lessons they feel they've learned. In the following chapter, I illustrate what they shared. It is definitely worth a read.

Chapter 19

IF I COULD DO IT AGAIN

n the beginning of this book, I shared the perceptions others had of me before my eyes were opened to a new, better way of living and before I knew how to become a person capable of creating it. If you recall, you read descriptions of me including low confidence, grouchy, a have-not, invisible, skeptical, opinionated, and judgmental. It only makes sense to share with you the perceptions others have of me now so you can identify the differences for yourself. You'll see these throughout this chapter.

Truly, this is not about making myself look good or inflating my ego. It is my effort to provide evidence I practice what I preach. I do not appreciate hypocrisy. I'm not sure I'll ever understand why anyone would not be a person of his word. I would never teach something I do not believe in myself. I feel strongly about every concept presented in this book, because they have all added to the quality of my life and my ability to help others with the quality of theirs.

Aaron Ball was mentioned earlier in this book because he was so good at standing out from the crowd from a young age. When he was in college, he came to work in my sales office during summer break. He knew it would give him great experience to add to his already above-average resume. I was happy to have Aaron on my team, because he was a sharp guy, a hard worker, and totally coachable. He was the highest producing rep on our team that summer and one of my favorite people to mentor. We developed a great relationship, still keep in touch and keep each other posted on professional opportunities. When I asked him for his opinion of me, here was his reply.

"Don't let her compact size or cool demeanor fool you. Amiee commands a room and has a brilliant low-key approach to leadership that draws out the personal best of each person on her team. She is able to coach to performance goals better than 99% of motivators I know. I could always count on her extreme honesty and realism." –Aaron Ball, founder of Ballpoint Communications Group

What do you want people to say about you? What reputation are you inspired to build?

Growth is an ever-present process. No matter how much we grow in some areas, there will always be other areas we can improve. Every experience we have teaches us something, and every person has experiences every day. While coaching new business owners, I had weekly conversations with Nick. He and I share a passion for continued improvement in business, and we found that passing ideas back and forth led to much better solutions than working on them individually.

"When I think of Amiee, I think of a compassionate individual hungry for personal and professional growth! One that goes above and beyond for others' needs. I can remember an infinite number of times that Amiee has impacted my life and my business in a positive way. She is funny, caring, and passionate about everything she does."

–**Nick Matlack**, business owner, recruiter, and sales manager

When you think about the people you've known for years, you can ponder how they've changed over time. Some changes are obvious to others, and some are only apparent when shared verbally.

It's true my family still struggles financially, and most of them lack the desire to make healthy decisions when it comes to tobacco, nutrition, and exercise. Nonetheless, they have made progress. I can't say whether that progress is by way of simply maturing with age or if it rode the coattails of several tough experiences leaving behind unforgettable life lessons. Either way, I can say with certainty—if my mom, dad, step-mom, step-dad, or brother could go back and do things differently, they would. We have all become closer and wiser over the years. Sadly, their clear remembrance and understanding bestows this reality:

You only get one life, and the clarity of purpose that may come to you in your forties, fifties, or sixties cannot make up for time squandered in your teens, twenties, or thirties.

Each would tell you to not follow in their footsteps and, instead, to implement the techniques in this book as early as possible so you can live your awesome life sooner rather than later.

My Dad Shares Lessons Learned

My father, who was taken out of school after eighth grade to help with the family work, never did receive any further formal education. He went on to serve as a marine in Vietnam where he lost many friends from his platoon, experienced some truly horrific times, and returned to the U.S. to be spit on by protestors of the war. Afterward, he married my mom, had two kids, got divorced, married my step-mom, got divorced again, and has since decided to fly solo. He has driven an eighteen-wheeler for more than thirty years and spends at least 300 days of the year on the road.

When I asked him what he'd do differently if he could turn back the clock, his answer was, "Pretty much everything." When I asked for specifics, he said, "I would have communicated—really communicated—in my first marriage. We had a serious failure to communicate."

He went on to add, "I wouldn't have let all of those people over the years live with us." He's referring to the multitude of people who moved in when they asked for his help, and he agreed to give them a place to live if they helped take care of us kids while he was on the road. They came and went like fads—some staying longer than others. As we grew up and no longer needed the live-in sitters, they became people that moved in just because they needed help. He finished by saying, "I would have made them make it on their own. They would have been stronger for it."

The change I've noticed in my dad that has strengthened our relationship is his openness. When I was younger, I'd ask him about his pre-parent life and his military experience, and he never wanted to talk about it. I continued to inquire, and over the last few years—now in his sixties—he has shared his history with me. Those conversations were memorable and made me feel closer to him than ever before.

Feeling the impact his openness had on me, I realized I could have that same impact on others. When I began working on my communication skills, I kept honesty and generosity at the top of the list when deciding how I'd share my experiences with people. Robert is one of those people. He was part of the mastermind group of young professionals for which I coordinated meetings and delivered messages.

"Amiee is always giving of herself and considerate of other people. She possesses an eternal optimism and is extremely helpful and organized. She has always been a great friend both personally and professionally."
—**Robert Danbury,** CUTCO Sales Professional

My Mom Shares Life Lessons

I'll begin the story of my mom with her first husband and child when she was sixteen. The baby died only six hours after birth due to a heart defect, and if dealing with that pain wasn't enough, she also suffered beatings and adultery at the hand of her spouse. She eventually had enough and left.

Years later, she met my dad and they were married shortly thereafter. She was eight years younger than my dad and not yet satiated in youthful merrymaking when she became a mother again. Their marriage only lasted four years and once my dad had custody of us kids, she was given a second chance to be carefree. She took it. Within three years, she was pregnant for a fourth time and walking down the aisle with her third husband.

When I asked her what she'd do differently, she said, "I'd have been a better mother; I would have taken more interest in my kids rather than in having fun and running around. I also would have made better decisions based on a long-term focus rather than just what felt good in the moment. As a young woman, I thought having a husband meant having someone to take care of me, so I didn't do things that would have given me the skills to take care of myself. That was a mistake. You never know when something awful could happen to your husband or his career, and it's scary to not have options."

When I was old enough to get a driver's license, my dad let me share his car. I'd drop him off at the trucking company where he'd pick up his semi and head out, and I'd use his car for school and work while he was gone. That fostered two things: my independence and my relationship with my mother. Since she had not spent a lot of time with us as kids, I started driving over to visit her. We have built a much stronger relationship since then, and I believe she is a much better mother than she displayed while we were young.

My Step-dad Shares Life Lessons

My mom is still married to her third husband more than twenty years later. She went through tough times dealing with his alcoholism, DWIs, and car crashes. It seemed there was no hope of him ever putting down the bottle until the day it landed him in the hospital suffering a heart attack.

He is now a recovering alcoholic. He has been sober since the day his heart nearly gave out, and here is what he had to say when I asked him what he's learned from his life experiences, "I would have lived for God and never started partying and drinking. After high school and the navy, I would have taken courses to get a higher education. I kind of thought I'd live forever, and there would always be time for that stuff, so I just lived for what was fun now. Then I went into factory work thinking that would last until I retired. When manufacturing took a huge hit in our area, I was out of a job for a long time, and I didn't have any skills to find something different."

My Step-mom Shares Life Lessons

My dad's second wife went through troubled times before, during, and after her marriage to my dad. She suffered molestation by the man who did the same to me years later. She struggled in a dysfunctional marriage and family when she became our step-mom almost immediately after my parents' divorce, and she went through subsequent years of angry fighting.

After she and my dad divorced, she was in a position in which she felt an attachment to kids whom she had no legal right to see, and she had a group of friends whose time was mostly spent drinking alcohol and doing drugs. She remarried and found herself in a relationship where pot was the chief component of their lives. I did visit her on occasion after she divorced my dad, but pot was always around, and I hated it. It had a severely negative effect on our relationship.

Things started to change when her best friend died in a car accident. While listening to the eulogy, her heart was touched significantly by the nun who delivered it. She decided that day, "Life can be over at any moment and it's worth more than sitting around and doing nothing."

She implored her husband they make considerable changes, but he was not interested. After many unsuccessful pleas, and a night in which he was supposed to pick her up from work, got high with a group of friends, forgot her, and she walked home for miles in the pouring rain, she decided to divorce him. She loved her husband and thought he was a good person, but he was using drugs daily with a life going nowhere positive, so she made the tough decision to strike out on her own. She stopped smoking completely; even moving away so she wouldn't be hanging around the same people or places that would provide temptation for it. "I even had to cut ties with my step-son, because he was a heavy drug user and I couldn't have it around me or my family. That was one of the hardest decisions I had to make."

She joined the Catholic Church, and after some time there, she met a man, and they became friends. They didn't go out on dates; they just talked on the phone for a year and fell in love while doing so. Eventually, they married and went on to adopt two girls. She says, "Every area of my life is happier now. My body feels and looks better now that I'm no longer smoking. It was boring at first when I left my friends and partying, but then life got better. I eventually had to just admit to all of my mistakes and let go of the guilt." She also learned the man that molested her wasn't her biological father, which lifted some of the burden of that experience, and she gained many new, loving family members once she found her real father.

She has built a superior life for herself, improving in all areas. Of all people close to me, I believe she has implemented the most positive changes. Recently, she has been a great example of not only progressive behaviors but also an empowering focus and a thick skin. She was diagnosed with a pretty serious illness that will lead to an organ transplant. Before the surgery can take place, she has some wellness tests she will have to pass that are requiring her to make nutrition and health decisions that would be challenging even for the healthiest people I know. With all of the challenges and the sacrifices she is making now, her attitude is one of optimism and personal responsibility. It is inspiring. Like me, her life and attitude now are vastly different than they were when she was holding herself back from greatness.

My Brother Shares Life Lessons

My brother was our most rebellious member of the immediate family. He had the same upbringing as I did—the trailer park, the cockroaches, the divorced parents, and the poverty—but the similarities end there. He hated school and authority whereas I flocked to it. He was a sexual being whereas I was closed off. He was a heavy drug user whereas I was drug free.

In his early teenage years, he skipped school so often that he ended up on probation for that offense alone, but that is where all of his legal troubles began. Once on probation, he was required to do check-ins and pass drug tests, both of which he failed to do. He went from huffing paint fumes to smoking marijuana to harsher fixes from crack and methamphetamine.

Once addicted, he and our family suffered many ill effects. More than once, he cleaned us out of our possessions—what little we had—to sell them for drug money. Once, my dad came home to find his car sitting on blocks after the tires had been removed and sold. As my brother moved from harsh drug to harsher drug, he also moved from detention centers to jail to prison. The charges were always related to drug possession or theft of the things he used to fund the habit. Along the way, he had two children—both girls, by different women. His lifestyle caused his absence from me when we were kids and his absence from his children in his adulthood.

Today, he is drug free. After the last prison sentence was served and he realized his girls were growing up without him in their lives, he chose to make the necessary changes. He recently married a hard working, drug-free, responsible single mother. My brother is the kitchen manager and main cook of a locally owned restaurant in his area, and he looks happier and healthier than I've ever seen him.

When I asked him what he learned or would do differently if he could go back, he said, "I would not have been a monster of society—tweaked out and causing trouble. I wasted so much time and money on doing drugs just because it was fun. It affected my kids, I missed time with them, and it hurt my family. It wears you down eventually. Instead, I would have applied myself in school, probably gotten a higher education. I also would have been a good father and had my daughters with me." (He currently has visitations with them.)

When I asked what advice he has for others, he said, "Don't do drugs. And you get out of life what you put into it. Look at my sister—you give 110% and you get 110% back. You put in good, you get good back. If you give heartache, you get heartache in return."

This concept hit me in my teenage years. I somehow knew I was the only one who could get myself to a better place. I couldn't wait for someone else to do it for me or wait for luck to strike. Knowing that what I put in would determine what I got out, I decided to work as hard as I could. And for the next ten years, I did.

Loyd was my mentor and supervisor for more than five years, and he was the top executive in the office in which I worked.

"Some of the things I appreciate about Amiee are her inexhaustible work ethic, her ability to find a way to solve any challenge, and her fearless approach to take on challenges without being limited by doubt or fear. She has great energy and a strong sense of integrity. I can't think of many others that I could entrust any part of my personal or professional life to and not be worried—knowing it would be handled with the same care and attention that I would give myself."

—**Loyd Reagan**, Region Manager, Vector Marketing Corporation

The First Time We Were All in the Same Room

Most of my life, my parents all fought with each other, my brother was unruly, and I wouldn't say any of them created the type of environment in which one finds happiness. When I got married, I was apprehensive about the wedding, because my husband's family of normal people—a mother who was an ER nurse for three decades and a father on the police force and their kids and relatives—would meet my family.

My husband grew up in a two-parent family, with dogs and cats, and a big house. At our wedding, they would meet my whole family, which at that time, had never all been in the same room together and were still filled with hostilities over previous disagreements. He'd have his mom, dad, and brothers, and I'd have my dad, my mom and her alcoholic husband, my sister and her children, my brother fresh out of jail, and my step-mom, her new husband and new family—a new family none of us had met yet. I couldn't fathom what they'd think of my motley crew.

To my surprise, it was a great event. No one fought, and people in my family, who hadn't spoken in years, had friendly conversations. Everyone had fun, and when the preacher asked if anyone had reason to object to our union, his family stayed quiet. Score!

My wedding day kicked off both the beginning of my life with my better half and a new, calmer family dynamic. These days, there is less animosity between my family members. We get along, and we recognize we share two things—past mistakes and insights imparted by hard life lessons. After all, a mistake made once is natural, but the same mistake made again and again is nonsense. Mistakes are for learning, not repeating.

Once you've taken time to reflect on the lessons you've learned through your own trials or tribulations, share your stories with others. Also be a seeker of stories, because they are great sources for knowledge. None of us has enough time to make all of the mistakes ourselves, so it's smarter to learn from others' experiences. Then use what you've learned personally and from others to become your awesome self, because besides your own gains, it can have a positive impact on your friends, family, and community.

Marianne Williamson, a *New York Times* Bestselling author and internationally acclaimed lecturer, said it well when she said, "As we let our own light shine, we unconsciously give other people permission to do the same."

A FUN STRATEGY FOR ACHIEVEMENT

Chapter 20

t's been said the world changes at a faster rate now than ever before. Though I never thought about it before, when I heard that, it seemed unquestionable. Just the past thirty years have brought us many firsts and most of them have given us some effective resources to use on our journey to awesome.

The first hand-held mobile phone was used in 1973 by its inventor. It weighed two and a half pounds and took ten hours to charge. In the last twenty years, cell phones have become an indispensable, common part of our lives and on average weigh less than five ounces. How does having a phone to use at any moment add to the awesomeness of your connections with others? I love making appreciation calls or texts to those who have impacted me positively any time it pops into my head.

In 1982, the first national snowboard race was held in Suicide Six, Vermont. Now snowboarding is a primary winter sport. That same year, the CD was introduced and changed the way we record and listen to music. Late in the 1980's, the HP-150 was created—the first computer with a touch screen. Of course, now touch screens are widespread with the addition of iPods, tablets, and smart phones. I think it is awesome to be able to simply touch a screen in order to work these products.

The mid-1990's brought us Windows 95, the internet started to gain popularity, Google was launched, the first keyless entry smart key was introduced, and the first hybrid vehicle—the Toyota Prius—became available. Can you think of anyone that doesn't have keyless entry? And now the question thrown around on occasion is, how would we survive if we ever lost the internet? That would not be awesome.

Google helped make the internet the place we go to find information— sorry, library. In 2004 and 2005, we were given the iPod—forever changing the way we carry and enjoy our music collections—and Facebook and YouTube. Facebook is the largest social media site in the world and YouTube gave us our first video sharing platform.

Imagine this, You have to put your key in the car door to unlock it, wait until you get home to call a friend, actually *call* your friend rather than text, and find any information you need without the use of the internet or the web. How different would your life be? It wasn't that long ago people lived exactly that way, and I'm guessing you think that sounds pretty not awesome.

In 2012, the three most visited websites were Facebook, Google, and YouTube. You may be one of those people old enough to drive a car but unaware of what life was like without a cell phone, GPS, or daily internet browsing. Maybe you can't fathom having to listen to music via cassette tape, record player, or even CDs. I hired an assistant recently—a junior in college—and when I asked her to send some thank you cards for me, I found out she had never sent anything by postal mail before. We had to discuss the proper way to address an envelope. I was shocked she lacked this knowledge, because she is a smart girl. Apparently, it's just not as relevant to her world anymore.

The point is the world changes rapidly. The question is will you change along with it or just stand by wishing you didn't need to? No matter the pace of progress going on around us, it is our choice how quickly *we* grow. Just think of all that you've accomplished or improved already just by reading these chapters and completing the exercises at the end of each. Reading this book is a first step, just like searching the web can find you helpful information or watching a video can teach you a new technique. However, until you put it to action, you won't experience the delight that accompanies growth.

In his movie, *The Art of Flight*, Travis Rice, possibly the most talented snow boarder to exist up to now, said, "Our lives have become digital and everything you could ever want to know is just a click away. Experiencing the world through second-hand information isn't enough. If we want authenticity, we have to initiate it." After watching his movie, I have no doubt that Travis knows how to have fun and has found his own Destination Awesome.

Change Begins with One Person

It blows my mind when I think of the changes in our world in a few short decades. It's more important than ever that we continue to develop ourselves so we can adapt and seize new opportunities.

The awe-inspiring part of history is every one of those accomplishments began with one person, with one idea. Other than time, nothing and no one moves forward without a person deciding to make progress.

W. Clement Stone, a poor boy who sold newspapers at 6-years-old, owned his own newsstand by 13-years-old, and went on to be a self-made millionaire and subject of the autobiography *The Success System That Never Fails*, once said, "Little hinges swing big doors." My interpretation is small changes can yield large results. All of the ideas covered in this book are just small shifts in perspective or action: being mindful of the connections in your life, making choices that will help you reach your goals, and continuing to learn and grow.

Anyone with a desire to improve an area of his existence can implement them today, in 600 seconds, and begin moving toward his goal. The following is a summation of the main topics and what will help you get to your own Destination Awesome.

Choose wisely when deciding with whom to spend your time.

Be trusting and trustworthy.

Positively affect others.

Look for good and strengths in others, and be open to learning from them.

Choose your identity and design your environment to align with it.

Get mentors who are successful in areas in which you'd like to improve.

Be productive with some of your time off in order to get more done.

Act in spite of fears.

Stand out from the crowd; strive to be better than average.

Develop a thick skin so setbacks and criticism won't deter you.

Focus your thoughts on empowering content.

Be aware of your self-talk and align it with your intent.

Position yourself for what you want.

Make the necessary sacrifices.

Changes in our world are inevitable, but outside of aging, a person changes by choice. Some or all of these success tips may be new to you, and if so, that is more advantageous than you may realize. Brendon Burchard said, "After peering into thousands of people's brains with advanced imaging machines such as the MRI, neuroscientists have concluded that the brain is hardwired to seek and enjoy novelty and challenge. Your brain becomes much more activated when something novel (new) or challenging occurs. Novel things make your mind snap to attention and become sharp, releasing dopamine and energizing your brain to go into 'let's figure this out' mode. And an engaged brain is a happy brain."

Even if the ideas I've shared are not new to you, it's still constructive to implement them in a new way, so if you haven't completed each of the action steps at the end of the chapters, consider going back to them. If you have completed them, take a moment to reflect on how far you've come. It confirms you are moving toward a destination fitting of your commitment. In any case, do not fear the unknown. Embrace it as an enhancement to your mental health.

The Fun of Firsts and Bests

In addition to the positive neuroscience behind it, doing things for the first time is both exciting and memorable. Do you remember your first kiss? Without a doubt. Do you remember your thirtieth? Probably not. Do you remember your first time on a roller coaster? Your first public speech? Your first sale? A child's first word? I continue to live for firsts. I didn't always realize it, but I know it now.

My jobs kept me interested as long as I was learning and growing. When I felt I was no longer making progress, I'd lose interest and look for a new position. It isn't only career-related. Being drawn to new things is partly why I jumped out of planes, rafted on white waters, hiked various trails, and embarked on many other adventures. They allowed me to confront fears and introduce fresh experiences simultaneously.

If you already know which new ideas in this book you want to utilize, don't hesitate. Take action now. Don't let another day go by without taking at least one small step. That step will lead to the next, and so on, and those footprints will be a record of your progress toward your awesome destination.

Once you've decided to take action, I've found the most fun strategy to be devising a plan to have some *firsts* and *bests*. If you're aiming for something you've yet to experience, then you'll be going for a first. Will it be the first time you've been the lead on a class or work project? The first time you attend a campus function? The first time you take a fitness class? The first time you defuse a nuclear weapon with only three seconds left on the timer? You haven't done that yet? Take your first drama class and maybe you'll get your chance.

If you're aiming to improve in something you've already done or are involved in, you'll be going for a best. Will it be your best sale or most awesome sales campaign yet? The most weight you've ever lost? Will you have your most intimate conversation yet? Will you read more than you've ever read in one month?

Here's your final Gone In 600 Seconds action step. Write down an experience you want to have that will be a first for you and a personal best you will shoot for. So you'll have two things written down—a first and a best.

I am honored you devoted time to reading about my history, my growth, and the lessons I've learned. You can use the ideas shared to help yourself and to help others. I do what I can to make sure no one I care about ever has to experience a family holiday like my fries and soda Thanksgiving, and since I've gained all of these tools in my tool belt, I am more successful in that endeavor. If you want to impact others, it's like they say on an airplane: put your own oxygen mask on first, then assist those around you.

I am grateful to have the opportunity to play a small role in your search for answers. I have worked closely with hundreds of people from all walks of life and been fortunate to witness their progress and cheered as they created awesome lives. I know you are capable of creating the life you desire. I know, because I've had conversations with people, read many stories of people, and coached people who chose to improve. And triumphed. They did what so many fail to—they went for it. Someone once said, you miss 100% of the shots you don't take.

Don't sit on the sidelines of your life. Be the star player.

You are awesome. Now go create the awesome life you want.

Quick Reference for

YOUR JOURNEY TO
DESTINATION AWESOME

Major Philosophies:

- You can have the life you desire—an awesome life—no matter the circumstances from which you began or are currently in.
- The routes to your awesome life are the Road Paved in Relationships, The Path of Personal Characteristics, and the Boulevard of Behavior.
- The world is always changing. Having connections, making good choices, and continuing to grow are the best ways to succeed in and adapt to those changes.
- The journey never ends because there is no limit to awesomeness. See the *Destination Awesome Action Guide* for actions and resources to use in addition to this book.

Destination Awesome Action Guide

- Download the *Destination Awesome Planning Guide* to have a resource to help you with mapping out a plan to achieve any goal. http://amieemueller.com/planning-guide-by-destination-awesome/

- Join the Destination Awesome Facebook community where you can interact with likeminded peers, post your ideas and questions, celebrate your wins and be inspired. Search Facebook for Amiee Mueller – Destination Awesome.

- Visit www.AmieeMueller.com where you can read more stories, share your own story, get free resources, send me any questions you have at ASK AMIEE, and/or sign up to be on our scholarship list.

- Read any or all of the following—books and magazines (not in any particular order) that have helped me
  - *SUCCESS* magazine
  - *The Happiness Advantage* by Shawn Achor
  - *15 Invaluable Laws of Growth* by John Maxwell
  - *The 21 Irrefutable Laws of Leadership* by John Maxwell
  - *The Last Lecture* by Randy Pausch
  - *How to Win Friends and Influence People* by Dale Carnegie
  - *The Rhythm of Life* by Matthew Kelly
  - *The Five Love Languages* by Gary Chapman
  - *The 4-Hour Work Week* by Timothy Ferriss
  - *The Seven Habits of Highly Effective People* by Stephen Covey
  - *Living College Life in the Front Row* by Jon Vroman
  - *The Miracle Morning* by Hal Elrod
  - *Rich Dad, Poor Dad* by Robert Kiyosaki
  - *Think and Grow Rich* by Napolean Hill
  - *The One Thing* by Gary Keller with Jay Papasan
  - *The Entrepreneur Rollercoaster* by Darren Hardy

Summary of Action Steps from Each Chapter:

- Make a list of any changes you'd like to make over the next six months.

- Write out a reframed perspective on a past experience that still affects you negatively.
- Send messages to 5 to 10 people asking for their opinions on your good qualities and areas for growth.
- Brainstorm two lists: the ways your peers affect you positively and the ways your peers affect you negatively. For a list of ideas, see http://amieemueller.com/peer-pressure-or-peer-power/
- Check out the list of acts of kindness at http://amieemueller.com/intentional-acts-of-kindness and choose seven (1 to do each day for the next seven days or 7 to do in one day).
- List of the 5-10 people close to you. Next to each name, write out 1-3 strengths they possess.
- Go back to the list you made of the changes you'd like to make in the next six months. Next to each change, put a name of someone who is successful in that area. Seek a mentor from that list.
- For the areas that rate the lowest on the trust scale, brainstorm why you rate it at that number and what you can do to improve in that area.
- Think about what you want your identity to be and write it down.
- List any and all fears that are keeping you from doing what you want. Decide which one you will battle first by acting anyway, and put a date next to it.
- Make two lists: #1—write down 10 accomplishments of which you are proud. #2—Write down 1 – 3 goals you'd like to accomplish in the next six months and why.
- If you don't have one, create a to-do list. If you have one, update it.
- Look over your identity description or make a list what you like about you, and underline of any characteristics you've held back or kept hidden in order to blend in.
- Make a list of all of the positive inputs you will use to direct your mind toward empowering thoughts. For examples, see http://amieemueller.com/constructive-inputs-will-feed-your-brain/
- Make a list of things that make you smile and/or laugh.

- Make a list of three things you want to achieve (in any time frame). Then brainstorm ways to position yourself for those goals.
- Make a list of any sacrifices you need to (and are willing to) make in order to create the life you desire.
- Write down an experience you'll work toward that will be a first for you, and write down a personal best you are going to go after.

BIBLIOGRAPHY & REFERENCE GUIDE

Chapter 1

Hard Times, College Majors, Unemployment, and Earnings. Georgetown University, Georgetown Public Policy Institute, Anthony P. Carnevale & Ban Cheah, May 2013.

Intergenerational Social Mobility: The United States in Comparative Perspective, Emily Beller and Michael Hout, Fall 2006. http://amieemueller.com/destination-awesome-book-reference-guide/

American Exceptionalism in a New Light: A Comparison of Intergenerational Earnings Mobility in the Nordic Countries, the United Kingdom and the United States, Forschungsinstitut zur Zukunft der Arbeit Institute for the Study of Labor, January 2006.

Chapter 2

15 Inspirational Rags-To-Riches Stories by Eric Goldschein and Dana Eisenberg | Dec. 28, 2011. http://amieemueller.com/destination-awesome-book-reference-guide/

Chapter 4
Larry Winget, *You're Broke Because You Want To Be* (Gotham, 2008)

Chapter 5
Shawn Achor, *The Happiness Advantage* (Crowne Business, 2010)
Inquiry: Critical Thinking Across the Disciplines, Linda Elder, Winter, 1996.
Vol. XVI, No. 2. http://amieemueller.com/destination-awesome-book-reference-guide/

Chapter 6
SUCCESS magazine, Homeless to Happyness, May 2008. Chris Gardner story.
SUCCESS magazine, Famous Failures, October 2013. Norman Vincent Peale story.

Chapter 8
In Brief: Fact Sheet, Guttmacher Institute, Facts on American Teens' Sexual and Reproductive Health, February 2012, SEXUAL ACTIVITY.
The Currency Of The New Economy Is Trust, Rachel Botsman, TED.com, June 2012

Chapter 9
SUCCESS magazine, Legend Series, Shoot for the Moon, August 2009. Les Brown story.
Brendon Burchard, *The Charge* (Free Press, New York, NY 2012)
The Secret to Getting a Job after College by Larry Chiagouris. Brand New World Publishing, 2011.
Katy Perry: Part of Me, 2012 Documentary, Insurge Pictures, MTV Films, Imagine Entertainment, Perry Productions, Direct Management Group, AEG Live
EMI Music, Pulse Films, Magical Elves Productions, Splinter Films

Chapter 10

SUCCESS magazine, Your Personal Best, Climbing Blind, April/May 2008. Erik Weihenmayer story.

SUCCESS magazine, Lessons From Sports, Pushing Past The Fear, June 2009. Laird Hamilton story.

Chapter 11

Weekend Edition, NPR, December 2012. One Direction Interview

John C. Maxwell, *The 15 Invaluable Laws Of Growth* (Center Street, New York, NY, 2012)

Famous People Who Found Success Despite Failures by Benny Hsu
    http://amieemueller.com/destination-awesome-book-reference-guide/

5 Tips To Developing Thicker Skin by MARGARITA TARTAKOVSKY, M.S
    http://amieemueller.com/destination-awesome-book-reference-guide/

How To Develop A Thicker Skin by Scott H Young
    http://amieemueller.com/destination-awesome-book-reference-guide/

The Thick Skinned by Lybi Ma, published on September 01, 2004
    http://www.psychologytoday.com/articles/200410/the-thick-skinned

Chapter 12

The American Institute of Stress, Workplace Stress,
    http://amieemueller.com/destination-awesome-book-reference-guide/

Chapter 13

National Center for Health Statistics. Health, United States, 2011: With Special Feature on Socioeconomic Status and Health. Hyattsville, MD. 2012.

Graduate Kyle Clarke nets a great job, by Joanne Butcher, The Journal. Dec 14, 2010. http://amieemueller.com/destination-awesome-book-reference-guide/

TV viewing at 'all-time high,' Nielsen says. By Taylor Gandossy. CNN.com
    http://amieemueller.com/destination-awesome-book-reference-guide/

Chapter 14

SUCCESS magazine, Improving Your Most Important Relationship in Life, October 2008. Robert Stuberg.

One dead after swimmers caught in Pass-A-Grille rip currents, FOX13TampaBay, June 27, 2012.

http://amieemueller.com/destination-awesome-book-reference-guide/

Teen dies, another in critical condition after swimming accidents in Gulf Shores surf, Mark R. Kent, Press-Register, April 18, 2012.

http://amieemueller.com/destination-awesome-book-reference-guide/

Chapter 17

U.S. Census Bureau, Statistical Abstract of the United States: 2012

Broke And Getting Broker: 22 Jaw Dropping Statistics About The Financial Condition Of American Families. March 29th, 2011. The American Dream.

http://amieemueller.com/destination-awesome-book-reference-guide/

Chapter 20

The Art of Flight, Brain Farm Digital Cinema, 2011. Starring Travis Rice.

CPSIA information can be obtained at www.ICGtesting.com
Printed in the USA
LVOW06s1849081015

457485LV00008B/958/P